Survival Food Handbook

Provisioning at the Supermarket for
Your Boat, Camper, Vacation Cabin,
and Home Emergencies

Janet Groene

*"Be prepared for what?" someone once asked Lord Baden-Powell,
the founder of Scouting. "Why, for any old thing," he cheerfully replied.*

Mc
Graw
Hill
Education

McGraw-Hill Education

New York • Chicago • San Francisco • Lisbon • London •
Madrid • Mexico City • Milan • New Delhi • San Juan •
Seoul • Singapore • Sydney • Toronto

1 2 3 4 5 6 7 8 9 0 DOC 21 20 19 18 17 16

ISBN   978-0-07-183721-7
MHID   0-07-183721-3

e-ISBN   978-0-07-184140-5
e-MHID   0-07-184140-7

Photos by Gordon Groene unless otherwise stated

McGraw-Hill Education books are available at special quantity discounts to use as premiums and sales promotions, or for use in corporate training programs. To contact a representative, please visit the Contact Us page at http://www.mhprofessional.com/.

Dedication

To my parents Ida and Irving Hawkins, who taught me to have good food on hand for good times and bad. And to Gordon Groene, my soul mate and skipper, who navigated our years of good times ashore, aloft, and afloat.

Contents

Introduction

Why a Cookbook Without Fresh Foods?

The iconic motto, "Be Prepared," means different things depending on who, where, what, and why.

To my father, as a Scout leader, it meant bringing out Velveeta and saltines for supper when the skies opened and his woebegone troop had to hunker under their canoes instead of cooking spaghetti over a campfire. To my husband and me, preparedness aboard our sailboat meant enough supplies to cruise the remote reaches of the Bahamas for weeks without refrigeration.

In our RV travels it means having food on board for boondocking, breakdowns, or unexpected delays. In our suitcase travels it means having a small stash of snacks so we don't have to rely on an overpriced minibar. Back home, being prepared means having a reserve of water, food, and fuel in case of power outages, a burst water main, or other emergencies that have hit our neighborhood. At times we've also been stalled by illness, forced to delve into food reserves because we were just too sick to get to a grocery store.

Stuff happens. Boats run aground, break down, get becalmed and gale-bound, or are delayed by bridges that won't open. Campers may get stuck by forest fires or highway closures. Hunters, trappers, and

When you've found the perfect place, extra provisions allow you to stay as long as you like. (RIVA)

1

city folks get snowed in. Manhattan never sleeps, yet even the Big Apple experiences interrupted food, fuel, and water services after floods or power outages.

Disasters aside, there are many happy reasons for having food in reserve. Friends drop in, or you might decide to stay an extra week in your hunting lodge or mountain cabin. Spare food allows you to be spontaneous. You don't need a very large food reserve to make it through an impromptu weekend sleep-in or camp out.

Food preparedness is simply an insurance policy. If you need the stowed food supplies, you're covered. If you don't, donate them to a food bank at the end of the season, trip, or voyage.

Emergency organizations such as the Red Cross urge the public to keep food and water on hand for at least three days so you can fend for yourself until help arrives. Depending on your lifestyle you might decide to expand that three-day supply to three months or more. Stockpiling food is not just for doomsday survivalists. It is creative, challenging, and smart. For boaters, campers, and other adventurers, provisioning is a skill required by the sport.

If you think canned and packaged foods cost too much, taste awful, and aren't good for you, these recipes might give you hope. It's likely you'll use them in concert with fresh ingredients. Even when all fresh foods are gone, however, you'll have balanced and interesting meals available from your pantry, food lockers, and dry bilges. If nothing else, these recipes can help you rotate supplies so your pantry remains ready and relevant.

This book isn't about buying a year's supply of MREs to squirrel away and forget. It's about enjoying nutritious, varied, and attractive meals every day, even under difficult circumstances. In these pages you'll find recipes plus tips on fuel and water, which are also crucial to food preparedness.

Now, let's eat.

How to Use This Book

Based on my own experiences as a household cook as well as a camper, RV wanderer, and sailor who's lived off the grid for months at a time, here's how to understand my recipes.

- This book assumes you will have at least one backup way to cook. It also assumes you may lack refrigeration at least some of the time. Refrigeration units break down. Electricity fails. Batteries go dead. Stuff happens. See the Appendix for ways to bake without an oven and Chapter 12 for tips on what to do when the freezer fails.

- Stove burners, ovens, grills, and campfires vary greatly in the amount of heat they deliver. To be assured of food safety, especially when cooking meat or eggs, use an inexpensive instant-read thermometer.
- Pressure cooking is highly recommended. It stretches your fuel supply and saves precious time. The lock-on lid is a plus in case of spills when cooking in a boat underway. A pressure cooker can also be used as a canner and sterilizer.
- Spice blends such as rubs and curry powders differ widely. Many cooks prepare their own, often starting with freshly ground whole seeds and pods. Measurements in my recipes are just a start. Also, most canned and packaged foods have some seasoning of their own. Fine-tune seasonings to your own tastes.
- If you have fresh herbs, use one tablespoon chopped fresh in place of one teaspoon dried.
- If you have room to stow a high-quality solar cooker, it's best to get a sturdy, efficient, commercially made unit sized to your needs. Use it often to learn how it works in different seasons. You can find designs for homemade solar cookers on the Internet.
- As much as possible, buy shelf foods with no added salt. Most commercial foods are high in sodium; when you combine two or more such foods, sodium overload can result. You can always add salt to taste at the table.
- Many stored staples don't release their best taste and highest nutritional value until they are milled or ground. It's smart nutrition practice to stock wheat berries, oat groats, and other whole grains. You may also want to store whole coffee beans, spices, and seeds. Consider investing in a grain mill to make flour, and a mortar and pestle to make spice blends or grind nuts. A small manual or electric coffee grinder is useful for very small chopping and grinding tasks such as coffee, tea, medicinal blends, and spices.
- In this book "flour" refers to all-purpose (wheat) flour, but even that can vary in different parts of the world depending on the type of wheat and how it's milled. Moisture content varies with climate. If you mill your own flour, settings range from fine to coarse, a matter of personal taste. Many non wheat

flours are found in the super-market and they can add variety to the menu. If you or someone in your group suffers from allergies, be sure to stock appropriate alternatives.

- Saltines can sometimes be found in "export tins," especially in markets outside North America. The tin protects crackers from crushing, moisture, and bugs, but they aren't actually preserved. They can still become rancid in the unopened tin. The same applies to foods such as French-fried onions and crisp Chinese noodles. Keep them cool and dry and observe use-by dates.

- In any storage situation—especially boats, basements, or belowground storage—it's smart to label cans with a grease pencil (not an indelible marker), which won't wash off in a flood. In a boat, wet paper clogs bilge pumps and limber holes, so it's wise to remove paper labels, then mark cans with a grease pencil before stowing.

- A good can opener plus at least one spare is a must. You need one that will chew through corned beef cans with lost keys and sardine tins after the pull tab breaks off. A GI-style can opener is compact enough to wear on a key ring. This type is slow and hard to use but reliable in a pinch. You may also need special openers for special food storage containers or to open long-life grain bins.

- Vegetable oils differ greatly in nutritional value, flash point (beware the fire danger!), and expiration dates. It's a personal choice, but you may want a variety of oils in the pantry, from gourmet olive oil for taste to peanut oil for high-temperature frying.

Protecting Stowed Foods

- Canned foods degrade faster in hot areas, slower where it's cooler. Bottled goods in clear glass degrade more slowly if kept out of harsh light. Cans and jars should be protected from freezing, which can cause them to burst.

- All shelf foods should be kept dry, as cool as possible, and out of bright light. Depending on where you store foods, additional protection might be needed against water damage, rats, or breakage. Cardboard, cellophane, aluminum foil, and thin plastics are no barrier against roaches and rodents.

- One way to cushion glass jars and bottles against motion in a boat or RV is to cut off and save knitted sleeves and sock tops from worn-out garments.

About Product Expiration Dates

Dates on cans and packages are a guide but not necessarily a death sentence. Unlike wines, which can turn bad overnight, most canned foods lose nutritional value, color, and texture gradually while remaining safe to eat for months, sometimes years.

Terms such as "use by," "sell by," and "best by" all mean different things. Some are simply inventory aids for supermarkets and are unrelated to food safety. Shelf life varies greatly, from a fairly short life for tinned milk to years for some canned seafood. Survival foods are packed to last for up to 20 years.

They'll stretch to slip over containers of varying sizes and are washable. Although glass is heavier to carry, it's a better moisture barrier than most plastics and, most importantly, it's vermin proof.

- Aboard your boat or vehicle where supplies get jostled, bag each can individually in inexpensive plastic bags and/or cover pull tabs with a little tape. Pull-tab seals are easily broken. In seagoing boats, tins, and especially aluminum drink cans, should be stowed where they won't contact highly corrosive salt water.
- Corrugated cardboard is filled with cubbyholes that shelter roaches and other bugs. Leave cardboard boxes outside.
- Freezing flour, grains, and meal for 24 hours before stowing reduces the chance of finding hatchlings later.
- Supermarket butchers are happy to custom cut and package meats for the home freezer or home canner. Custom packaging eliminates bone, gristle, fat, and puffy plastic trays, saving you prep time and sometimes awkward waste.
- Square and rectangular storage containers are more space efficient than round.

A Glossary of Shelf-Stable Foods

Apples are available dried and freeze-dried, but one easy, economical way to buy shelf-stable apples in the supermarket is to look for canned, pie-sliced apples in water. Do not confuse them with apple pie filling,

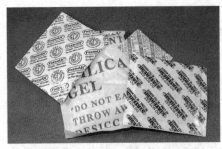

You've seen these small packets in commercial packaging. Some absorb moisture. Some absorb oxygen. Both have a place in some food storage programs.

which is heavily spiced and sugared.

Baby food can be a handy addition to recipes even if you don't have an infant. A fine purée, it stirs into batters, soups, and stews. A jar of carrot purée adds buttery glow to pancake batter; a jar of strained beets enriches chocolate cake. The small sizes make them handy for single use.

Baking powder begins to lose its oomph in about six months. To test it, stir a heaping teaspoon into a cup of water. If it starts to fizz at once, it's good.

Baking soda lasts indefinitely and it provides plenty of rising power when mixed with an acid such as buttermilk. Many recipes call for both baking powder and baking soda. Baking soda is also a food-quality abrasive, safer to use as a scrubber if you're on short water rations.

Beans, dried. Dried beans differ greatly, but as a rule of thumb a cup of dried beans swells to about 2½ cups cooked beans.

Black beans (*frijoles negros*) called for in this book are available canned or dried and are popular in Spanish cuisine. They should not be confused with fermented soybeans called black beans and used in Asian cooking.

Bouillon is an invaluable, concentrated flavor ingredient. It comes in powder, cubes, and pastes. The most common flavors are beef, chicken, and vegetable, but the alert shopper will also find it in ham, fish, tomato, and other flavors.

Browning is the term used in some recipes to refer to a deep brown-colored flavor enhancer sold under brand names such as Gravy Master, Kitchen Bouquet, and Bovril. Highly concentrated, it's a useful addition to the pantry shelf.

Bulgur is an ancient food. It's a precooked wheat that can be stirred into boiling water, covered, and left to "cook" itself off the burner. Use it as an alternative to instant rice.

Canned goods vary greatly in quality and in use-by dates. Before buying in case lots, compare brands for taste and texture. It's best to provision with salt- and sugar-free canned foods. You can always add sugar and salt later.

Dried beef, also called chipped beef, is on the best-buy list of storage foods for price, compact size, and versatility. It can be eaten cold, served in cream sauce, or torn into any soup or stew. A 2.25-ounce jar can serve a crowd if enough cream sauce is provided.

Ethnic foods add variety to the food shelf. When provisioning for the long term, shop every aisle of the supermarket even if you don't usually cook Indian, Hispanic, or Kosher meals. You're sure to find unusual and delicious foods to add variety to a stowed-food menu.

Fruit leather from commercial sources many also be called fruit taffy or fruit roll. It's another way to have fruit in the pantry, but read labels. Some are loaded with sugar or high-glucose syrup plus food dye or preservatives.

Garlic, Shakespeare's "stinking rose," is essential to cuisines around the world. Bulbs don't last long on the shelf or even in the refrigerator. Other forms of garlic are minced or whole cloves in jars, garlic salt, garlic powder, and garlic granules. Granules are coarser and take longer to rehydrate but provide a little more texture in a recipe.

Hams are preserved in many ways. Some hams don't require refrigeration. Some canned hams are shelf stable and some canned hams must be refrigerated. Some refrigerated, packaged hams are ready to eat; some require thorough cooking. Some must be soaked first. Read labels. Cured meats should be kept frozen for only one to three months. The salt in them hastens their breakdown even when frozen.

Honey keeps forever. It's used as a sweetener and a preservative, and it has medicinal uses. If it crystallizes, gently reheat to restore viscosity.

Instant soups that are made by the cup can be useful ingredients, especially for singles. Use a packet of cream of tomato to add a blush to a recipe. Add just enough water to cream of chicken soup to make a sauce or gravy.

Meats and seafood, canned. Recipes in this book call for canned ham, which may be whole or "formed," but is slice-able, and also for "chunk" ham, which is canned in pieces. The canning process softens most fish bones, such as salmon. They can be mashed and included in the dish if you wish. Canned, whole chicken contains tiny, brittle bones that are a hazard but difficult to remove. I no longer buy them and, when home-canning, use only boneless, skinless cuts. Canned tuna comes in "chunk" or a meatier "solid pack." It may be packed in water, oil, olive oil, or a flavoring ingredient such as tomato sauce.

Meat substitutes, usually made from soy, are a staple in some pantries, but not everyone likes them. Dried TVP (textured vegetable protein) comes in many forms to masquerade as ground beef, beef chunks, chicken, and so on. Experiment with different types and preparations to see if it has a place in your provisioning plan.

Milk substitutes should be considered, as many people suffer from dairy intolerance. Long-life alternatives are soy, rice, almond or oat beverages, and cream substitutes; you can sometimes find powdered soy milk in natural food stores.

Miso, a Japanese product made from aged soy and sea salt, is available in paste form or powdered sachets, and can be substituted for boullion.

Nonfat dry milk develops an "off" taste in hot temperatures. Keep it cool and observe use-by dates. It's popular with roaches and rodents—they can gnaw through cardboard/plastic/foil packages.

Oats/Oatmeal is one of the most economical, versatile, and nutritious foods in the larder. Cooking times depend on whether oats are whole (oat groats), steel cut, or rolled; rolled varieties include thin (one-minute) and thick (old-fashioned). Instant oatmeal requires only the addition of hot water. The less any grain is processed, the longer it takes to cook, but the more fiber and nutrition it provides.

Peanut butter is in the Top Ten of many provisioning lists—and allergens. Read labels to avoid spreads that contain sugar and other additives. "All natural" or "organic" doesn't necessarily mean that the peanut butter doesn't contain saturated oil, lard, sugar, or other unwanted ingredients. Alternative nut butters (almond, cashew) and seed butters are widely available.

Prunes, now sold as pitted dried plums, vary in moisture content. Some are very soft for snacking. Boxed prunes are moderately dry and require cooking. Prunes or dried plums packed for survival storage are very hard and dry. Liquids in recipes must be adjusted for the kind of prunes you're using.

Pumpkin. Do not confuse canned pumpkin, which is simply puréd pumpkin, with pumpkin pie filling, which has sugar and spices. Purée makes a delicious

Caribbean-style pumpkin soup and disappears into many other recipes, such as chili or stews.

Quinoa, another ancient grain, is a good substitute for bulgur or couscous if you do not use wheat products. It is often available in ready-made foil pouches.

Raisins are one of the supermarket's most affordable dried fruits.

Retort pouch foods have been around since the 1970s. They are lighter to carry. Foil pouches weigh less and take less room, especially in the waste bin. Also, shelf-stable meals are available in plastic and cardboard containers that can be heated in the microwave and eaten out of the package. They're ideal for an office lunch but impractical for provisioning because they're bulky in the cupboard and in the trash.

Rice is the prepper's best friend. Some 40,000 varieties are grown around the world in countless sizes, flavors, and colors. Shelf life differs. Get acquainted with all the ways to buy, store, and cook this invaluable resource.

Salt keeps for years if kept dry. Keep a supply of non-iodized or pickling salt on hand as an emergency preservative. Most of my recipes don't call for salt

Shelf-stable packets and pouches are light to carry. Consider cost, food quality, and how you'll dispose of the trash.

because canned and packaged foods are usually loaded with it. Add it to taste and, for a gourmet touch, experiment with the many specialty salts now in the marketplace.

Seeds can be used for sprouting, as an ingredient, and sometimes ground up and used as a flavoring ingredient. Nutrient rich, they are beloved by bugs and should be protected.

Serving dishes may already be in your boat, cabin, or camper. If you are selecting tableware for all-purpose emergency use, get shallow soup bowls or deep, rimmed plates. (Think pie pans.) Many of the best one-dish recipes are soups or stews. In emergencies you're likely to stretch scant supplies by adding more broth or water. Speckled metal enamelware, usually found in camping supply shops, has been an unbreakable camping classic since pioneer times.

Sesame seeds, also known as benne seeds, provide flavor and texture to a dish as well as fats, vitamins, and minerals. They come in white, black, or golden, each with their own characteristics. Known mostly as a garnish in American kitchens, they are a nutritional mainstay in some cultures. Tahini, or sesame paste, is a spread similar to peanut butter. Sesame oil is a flavor enhancer in Asian cuisine.

Smoke flavoring, also called liquid smoke, comes in a bottle and is used by the drop. It can last for years on the pantry shelf. It adds a meaty overtone to meals, but use it very sparingly. Too much turns a dish bitter and acrid.

Sugar keeps for years and is used as a sweetener and preservative. Sugar substitutes vary greatly in stow-ability and few can be used as preservatives.

Tofu (soybean curd) is available refrigerated, freeze-dried, dehydrated, and in shelf-stable packages. It can also be frozen or dried in a home dehydrator.

When a recipe such as quiche or custard pie calls for eggs, it's important to use fresh or reconstituted eggs that "set" as they cook, not freeze-dried eggs that are already cooked.

Water chestnuts come in cans whole, sliced, or diced. Use them for "crunch" in salads when you're out of fresh celery and other ingredients that add texture contrast.

Wine, liquor, and liqueurs can be used as flavoring and as a preservative (think rum cake). Wine is choosy about light and temperature. Handle with care.

Vinegar keeps for months, and even years, but it's best to stick with commercial apple cider vinegar and distilled white vinegar because of their reliable acidity. Homemade vinegar may not be acidic enough to use safely as a preservative. If you create flavored vinegar by adding herbs, make small batches and use them quickly because too many additions reduce the acidity, inviting spoilage.

Vitamin supplements have a place in some food-storage plans. Powdered multivitamin drink sachets or tablets mix with water and are very handy. Keep them cool, dry, and out of bright light. Observe expiration dates.

Freeze-Dried Versus Dehydrated

Suppliers of emergency foods offer both freeze-dried and dehydrated foods. Supermarkets also offer at least some shelf-stable choices, such as freeze-dried fruit snacks, dried vegetable soup mix, and dried meats such as jerky, pepperoni, and chipped beef.

Freeze-dried foods are more true to their original color and taste when rehydrated, but they are bulkier and cost more. Read directions for preparing these foods. Some require hydration plus cooking; some are ready to eat after being rehydrated with hot water.

When stocking dehydrated long-life foods from emergency food suppliers, note that they usually have a much lower moisture content than, say, prunes or dried apricots from the supermarket. It takes more time and water to rehydrate them.

Eggs are available dehydrated, freeze-dried "raw," and freeze-dried "cooked," as in omelets and scrambled eggs. Just add hot water and precooked eggs are ready to eat. However, they are already "set," so they don't work as an ingredient in custards and meat patties.

Janet Groene's Top 13 Foods for Storage

Rule One is to get as much food value as possible per ounce, per penny, and per cubic inch. These foods fulfill that promise, and many of them can probably also play a role in your daily cuisine.

Bouillon
Cheese
Dried chipped beef
Eggs, powdered
Emergen-C powdered fruit
    drink
Milk, powdered
Nuts, unsalted, in cans or jars
Peanut butter
Popcorn (unpopped)
Raisins
Rice
Rye crackers
Tomato paste

My Own Top Foods for Storage

_____
_____
_____
_____
_____
_____
_____
_____
_____

When provisioning to drive the Alaskan Highway, the Great Plains, or the Australian Outback, plan extra supplies.

Chapter 1

Food Readiness with Supermarket Staples

When food preparedness is an everyday fact of life, smart budgeting is important. You don't simply stash and forget long-life foods. You plan food supplies by the month, perhaps by the week; that means buying with economy and using shelf supplies often.

Let's look at what today's highly competitive supermarkets offer at everyday prices. Begin by shopping with fresh eyes. *Provisioning* is different from weekly shopping. When you take the time to shop aisles you don't usually see, you'll find many useful shelf foods.

A Tour Through the Grocery Store

The more you rely on pantry supplies, the more important variety becomes. Look at every aisle—including baby food and ethnic food departments. If you don't keep kosher or have never really explored Indian or Asian food, you usually breeze past these shelves. Now take

a second look and prepare to be pleasantly surprised. You'll find treasures such as a good Indian chutney or pickles, canned lychee fruit, and English marmalade. The aim is to eat according to current government guidelines, stay within budget, and keep the menu palatable.

Don't just assume that anything goes because you're starving and

Look at supermarket shelves with new eyes and be amazed at the variety of shelf-stable foods available to stock a prepared pantry.

desperate. These foods are meant to be eaten, enjoyed, and replaced.

Beverages

If water is a reliable, renewable resource in your geography, there is no point in devoting space to ready-to-drink beverages. In your boat or RV, it costs fuel and space to haul cases of juices and soda. One way to save weight and space at home and on the go is with a homemade soda system, such as Soda Stream, made with plain water and flavor concentrates.

Drink powders and concentrates are available in many types and flavors. Many have vitamins and natural flavonoids. Some are sugar free. Tang, the powdered orange "astronaut" drink, has been readily available for generations. One of the most economical concentrates is tomato paste, which can be diluted to make tomato juice.

Whether to add alcoholic beverages to your provisions list is a personal choice. Some long-haul cruisers

Spirits are a time-proven way to preserve foods—Tortuga Cakes take the biscuit in this regard!

save space by carrying only 151-proof grain alcohol on board. Flavored and diluted, a little goes a long way.

Cereals, Pastas, Grains, and Dry Beans

The biggest "space hogs" in food storage are ready-to-eat cereals and puffy snacks such as crackers and chips. For the best nutrition and most compact storage, focus on oatmeal (especially steel-cut), barley, farro, corn grits, and a variety of rice.

As you shop, read labels and use-by dates. Then keep foods as cool and dry as possible and out of bright light. Whole grains contain oils, a good thing, but oils also attract vermin and hasten spoilage. Most dry items last longer if put in mylar bags with an oxygen-absorbing packet, also called an oxygen scavenger. Mylar bags and Oxy-Sorb aren't usually found in the supermarket but can be ordered online (see Appendix). Don't confuse oxygen scavengers with silica packets, which are desiccants or drying agents. Both have their use in food storage.

All-purpose flour has a long shelf life unless bugs get into it. Self-rising flour has leavening that shortens its shelf life. Biscuit mix and other mixes (including cornbread mix and some pasta and rice mixes) containing fat should be used even sooner. Because of added preservatives to stabilize fats, some cooks avoid these altogether.

Rice, couscous, and most beans and grains absorb all their cooking water. Pasta and dry noodles, by contrast, require large amounts of boiling water that is poured off. That wastes both cooking fuel and water. In any case, if pasta is a vital part of your provisioning plan, get better nutrition with whole wheat or multigrain varieties.

Dry beans, peas, and lentils are staples in many pantries and are a major source of protein in vegetarian and vegan diets. Because beans come in so many sizes and colors you can keep shuffling the deck for days without repetition: black beans and white rice, red beans and red rice, kidney beans and pasta, navy bean soup and cornbread, lentil stew, hummus, refried beans, ad infinitum.

In a fuel-short situation, split peas and lentils cook fairly quickly without presoaking. Other dry beans require more time and water. Both have a place in food storage. It's a good idea to stock some canned beans too. They're ready to eat even if you have no heat at all.

The Soup Aisle

Bouillon, it's said, was invented as a way for Napoleon's army to have a concentrated meat they could carry in a pack or pocket. Today it is still the prepper's friend, a highly distilled food that makes a bracing broth with nothing more than hot water. It's also a powerful flavoring ingredient. Thicken it to make gravy. Add it to soups and stews. Enrich pasta and beans by cooking them in bouillon rather than plain water. Just keep in mind that it's very salty, so go easy with the salt shaker.

If weight is a factor, forget liquid concentrates and broths in favor of bouillon cubes and powders. The most common bouillon flavors are chicken, beef, and vegetable, but tomato, ham, and fish cubes are found in most supermarkets. Ethnic food stores may carry even more flavors.

Ready-to-serve soups are a waste of space, but you may want to stock some condensed soups because they can be prepared with little or no heat. Instant soups and ramen may also fit in for speed and convenience.

Dairy

It's likely most items in this department are refrigerated, which means they should be kept cold. However, keep an eye open for shelf-stable items like displays of cheeses or salami hanging up in the open air. See Chapter 2 for tips on preserving butter and eggs.

The Deli Department

Designed for hurried shoppers seeking ready-to-eat foods, deli departments are filled with high-priced gourmet foods. Don't sail through without a peek! Intense flavors go a long way, and you may find a few specialty items to hang a ruffle on a meal.

Meat

Shelf foods you might find in the meat department include jerky, summer sausage, some precooked bacons, chitterlings (pork intestines or "chitlins"), and cracklins (deep-fried pork rind).

If you have refrigeration, shop here too for vacuum-packed meats like ham and salt pork with a use-by date many weeks away.

Pouches, cans, and jars of real bacon bits and crumbled bacon are a flavor explosion in a small, long-life package. Imitation bacon bits don't even come close, although they are a choice for vegetarians. In any case, sprinkle them on just before serving unless directions specify otherwise. In some recipes they lose their punch when cooked.

Dried and smoked fish, and salt cod in traditional wooden boxes, are commonly found in supermarkets in a refrigerated bin. Unrefrigerated salt fish (*bacalao*) might be available in your area.

There are many positive reasons for having extra food in reserve at home and on the go—the best one is when you can stretch the advantages of great weather and company.

Refrigerated canned hams have a very long shelf life but must be kept cold. To find canned ham that needs no refrigeration, move on to the canned meat aisle.

Paper Products, Cleaning Supplies

This book is about food survival so we won't go into all the paper products and personal supplies you may want to buy in these departments. When a food emergency sends you to the pantry shelf for a meal, some items are especially useful. They include trash bags for cleanup, heavy duty trash bags for waterproof storage, and aluminum foil for campfire cooking.

Plastics break down from heat and light; aluminum foil corrodes and crumbles, especially in sea air. Rotate these supplies at least every two years.

Keep extra chlorine bleach with food supplies for sanitizing. Extra baking soda is handy as a neutralizer and food-quality abrasive scrub. Detergents break down with time, so supplies should be rotated regularly.

Produce

Fresh fruits and vegetables are the last thing to load before leaving for your cabin at the lake, starting a cruise, or embarking on an RV trip. Keeping them fresh as long as possible is covered in Chapter 2. Shop earlier for shelf-stable foods; visit the produce department to find nuts, unpopped popcorn, dried fruits, minced and whole garlic preserved in jars, and perhaps dry seeds for sprouting.

Fats, Oils, and Vinegar

To satisfy the fats and oils category, find vegetable oils of many kinds plus olive oil in bottles or tins. Lard comes in cartons or plastic tubs. Regular and butter-flavor shortening comes in cans and in individual sticks packed in cartons like butter. Ghee, or clarified butter used in Indian cooking, can be found in ethnic grocers in tins or sachets and is by nature very stable.

Find vinegars next to oils. Choices range from gourmet balsamic vinegars to inexpensive white, distilled vinegar for use in recipes or as a cleaning aid.

Dairy, Non-refrigerated

On supermarket shelves find canned, powdered, and long-life dairy and nondairy milk, which is convenient but also the most heavy and bulky way to stow milk. Flavored coffee creamers add a nice touch to hot drinks and dessert recipes.

Look for Dulce de Leche (sweetened condensed milk) and tinned cream on supermarket shelves.

Individual Packaging, Yes or No?

The most wasteful way to buy foods is in individual packages, but don't rule them out completely. Single-serve packets cost more per portion and create waste—a major nuisance on boats and camping trips, when you must consolidate and pack out trash. On the plus side, they stay fresh longer, provide portion control, and help you plan. Say you're provisioning for seven breakfasts for four people. It's easy to count off individual cereal boxes or packs of toaster tarts.

Farm markets are often a good place to buy provisions.

About Farmer's Markets

Shopping at native markets is one of the great pleasures of cruising by boat or RV. Discover local specialties and heirloom varieties, and cook them in your own galley. Meet the growers. Buying farm-market foods for storage, however, has its drawbacks unless you know the vendors and what regulations are enforced.

Ask vendors if your choices are really organically grown. Are the eggs truly from free-range chickens? Can you believe that the dried fruits are sulphur free? Will the homemade hot sauce give you botulism or does the artisan cheese contain the bacteria listeria?

It's a huge plus when provisioning if you can find fresh eggs that have never been refrigerated, apples that haven't been in cold storage for months, and cabbages still snuggled in their protective outer leaves. Supermarkets rarely offer such things. See Chapter 2 for tips on buying fresh for the long haul.

Chapter 2

Extending Life of Fresh Foods

Supermarket Savvy

Many fresh supermarket foods fit into a long-term provisioning plan. When I'm gunkholing in a boat with no refrigeration I know that the ice will be gone in a few days. With it will go the lettuce and other delicate food. After that we'll go to cole slaw for a salad course since cabbage keeps in the open air for weeks. When boondocking in our RV, which has a small refrigerator and freezer, I fill them first but also make room

elsewhere for baskets of potatoes, bags of apples and oranges, hands of green bananas, hard honeydew melons, and some green tomatoes. As a result, fresh produce lasts up to a month before we go on a "shelf-food" diet.

Many excellent books are available on home canning, dehydrating, curing meat, and other food preservation methods. However, the focus of this book is provisioning that anyone can do in hometown supermarkets. Let's shop.

Melons can be stored now to ripen in a week or two; hard squash can last for weeks.
(Dana Styber)

Getting the Most from Produce

1. Buy seasonal produce at its peak.
2. Buy some items that ripen after picking, such as melons for the short term and green tomatoes and bananas for the longer term.
3. Wash and dry thoroughly unless you'd rather wash items just before use. (Keep in mind that later you may be skimping on water.)
4. Wrap each piece individually in a breathable, absorbent wrap such as tissue. I use paper towels for wrapping. They stay clean and dry, so they're used later as paper towels. Some items do better when stored in perforated plastic bags that allow breathing but also help retain moisture.
5. Store produce in a cool, low-light, well-ventilated area.
6. Pick over produce every few days. Gentle rotation occasionally may help prolong freshness, but the main value is to locate bad spots as early as possible. A telltale stain on the wrap tells you the item needs to be removed, trimmed, and used if possible.

Fruits and Vegetables

Some fruits and vegetables are better than others for storage. Gardeners often plan several varieties of crops such as potatoes or tomatoes so they'll have a rich harvest, from early "new" potatoes to heat-tolerant cherry tomatoes. Supermarket shoppers don't have that choice. The most important factor is how old the food was when you bought it. Eyeball, smell, squeeze. Know where the produce came from and when. Chat up the produce manager to learn the best days to shop. Most large chains have their own growers that supply produce to their own specifications.

If you've heard about a health scare or recall, ask a produce manager if it applies where you shop. After an outbreak of illness from cantaloupes was in the news, I made a friend when I asked our local produce manager about it. He was proud as punch to tell me that his buyers have their own sources and standards. He knew just where his melons came from, and when; I was assured that the recall didn't apply. Now I consult him often when I want to buy produce that will last longest.

Observe how the supermarket handles produce. Apples and potatoes that were slammed around won't show their bruises until you get them home. Are the market's bins kept clean and cool? Your nose knows.

Produce must be thoroughly dry before stowing. Experts don't agree on whether produce should be washed right after purchase. It's a personal choice. I fill a spray bottle with one part white vinegar to two parts water and add a drop (no more) of detergent per quart. (This helps the spray spread better.) Unlike cleaners made with bleach or soap, the vinegar spray is nontoxic.

In most cases, root vegetables are best left earthy. A layer of soil helps protect them. Leafy vegetables are also unwashed until just before they're eaten because it's almost impossible to dry them thoroughly.

Washed or unwashed, the goal is to keep produce cool, dry, and well ventilated. Remove plastic bags or at least fill them full of holes. Check for bugs and bruises. A popular way to store produce in the air is to hang it up in net bags. In a boat or RV, secure them against motion that could bruise produce. Some consumers swear by plastic "green bags" or disks containing a chemical said to retard spoilage. A popular option for cruising sailors is to wrap lettuce in one layer of clean paper towels and then in newspaper, which cushions it and keeps it dry.

Buying produce "green" will allow you to keep fruits and vegetables longer. Handy if you are going to be visiting a remote area for an extended amount of time. (Public Domain)

Waxed Produce

Waxes retain moisture and protect against bruising, but health-conscious consumers may want to buy only unwaxed, organic products. *World's Healthiest Foods*, is published by the non-profit George Mateljan Foundation with no commercial interests or advertising. If you buy items that are waxed, the group suggests asking the grocer what kind of wax is present. It could be a petroleum-based wax or something natural such as beeswax. The only way to remove either is to peel the product.

Fruits and vegetables most likely to be waxed are nonorganic bell peppers, eggplant, potatoes, apples, citrus fruits, cucumbers, and rutabagas. When paring them, take the thinnest possible layer to avoid losing prime nutrients that lie just under the skin.

Dairy

Fresh milk requires kid-glove handling, so don't buy more than can be kept cold and used before its expiration date. Some dairy and non-dairy milk is sold in supermarket refrigerated cases even though the use-by date is months away. Read labels. Compare different types and brands.

For everything else, look for the farthest-out expiration dates. Hard cheeses last longer than soft. Bricks of cheese last longer than

Buy eggs that are as fresh as possible and turn them regularly. For longer storage, rub shells with a food-quality sealer such as margarine.

sliced or shredded. Coated cheeses (brie, gouda) have an added layer of protection. Some gourmet cheeses may be preserved in oil or brine, or stocked and sold unrefrigerated. Ask the merchant how to best care for them.

Thanks to the popularity of home cheesemaking in North America, supplies for extending cheese life are easily found online. Look for cheese wax, cheese bags, and cheese paper. If you buy a large cheese, these specialty products help keep cut sides from spoiling before you can finish it.

Refrigerated Convenience Foods

Pizza dough is commonly available in supermarkets, usually in the dairy department or bakery. Follow storage instructions provided. Pizza dough *à la* Pillsbury is also sold in compressed tubes with an expiration date some weeks away. Also available in such tubes are biscuits, crescent rolls, bread sticks, and cinnamon buns.

Usually displayed with refrigerated, prepackaged lunch meats are fresh pastas, pasta sauces, and mashed potatoes. While not cost- or space-efficient, they're an option and will keep for some time under refrigeration. Check preparation instructions and use-by dates and keep them cold.

Beverages

Refrigerated juices, juice blends, and bottled smoothies are popular items in modern supermarkets, but many are not actually preserved. In fact, freshness is their selling point, which means they must be kept cold and used by their expiration dates. Read labels.

Refrigerator Basics and Needs

Most modern household refrigerators and some custom units in boats and vacation homes have different zones for different foods. Learn to use different sections and drawers to prolong freshness. Read the owner's manual to learn what the zones actually do, then put an inexpensive

refrigerator thermometer in each compartment for a 24-hour period to see how well they work in your environment.

Important: While you're getting acquainted with your refrigerator, make note of its electrical starting and running load. If you plan to keep it going with a generator or inverter during a power outage, this information can make or break the success of your backup plan.

A large family at the beach house are into the refrigerator every few minutes for snacks and cold drinks. In an RV or boat, a refrigerator may be subjected to broiling sun for hours each day. The fridge at your fish camp in the cool north woods may hardly run at all. The thermostat needs to be set for your personal usage.

Using zones allows you to keep the milk and meat cold without freezing delicate produce and cheeses. The meat drawer is designed to be very cold, perhaps by taking air directly from the freezer. Produce drawers, also called crispers, have adjustable vents that can be opened or closed to control humidity. The butter keeper is a little warmer and may be a good place to put medications that must be stored within a certain temperature range.

If the refrigerator and/or freezer fail, see the Appendix.

Chapter 3

Before You Start Shopping

When you are provisioning for the long term, your biggest puzzles are what to buy, how much is enough, and how to allocate resources in a way that nourishes body and spirit for as long as necessary.

When you're provisioning for a set period, preparation can be fairly precise. You may be planning food for three weeks of dry camping in Quartzite, Arizona, in an RV; a long winter in a remote Alaskan cabin; or a month-long voyage among uninhabited islands in the back of beyond. You simply forecast X meals over Y days. For insurance, add extra supplies for one day per week. That means planning eight breakfasts, lunches, dinners, and snacks per person for each week you'll be gone.

If you want to be ready for a rare home emergency such as a prolonged power outage, only you can decide how many days or weeks you can realistically prepare for. The American Red Cross suggests everyone have enough supplies for three days. Mormons are commanded to have a year's supply of food on hand.

Your own readiness program may lie somewhere in between.

It begins with your appetite for spending the time, space, and money required to plan and store food. A complete program also relies on your willingness to rotate supplies.

How Much Is Enough?

Serious preppers allot so many calories per person per day (usually 2000 kcal). Assuming a set consumption allowance, they then stow food for so many days. Mountain House, a major supplier of freeze-dried foods in long-life packaging, offers an "essential" three-day assortment that contains 7,690 calories (chili mac, spaghetti, and so on) and a "classic" assortment measuring 6,740 calories including some breakfast items.

My approach is more upbeat. Pantry foods are part of everyday life whether we are traveling by boat or RV or we are at home. Some of our favorite meals come from cupboard ingredients.

(continued)

Four Ways to Handle Food Rotation

It's a chore to keep your culinary cloverleaf flowing, but the rewards of faithful rotation are many. First, you save money by avoiding waste. Second, you constantly discover new recipes, new products, and new ways to provision and plan. One of these rotation routines may work for you.

1. Create a schedule for using stored foods regularly. For example, you might serve pantry foods for breakfast each Monday, lunch on Tuesday, and dinner every Saturday.
2. Use up large amounts of canned and shelf food by preparing recipes found in this book for every potluck, bake sale, and sick call. Don't forget to replace them with updated supplies.
3. Donate foods to a food bank at the end of the cruise or RV trip, or when you close up your fishing lodge at the end of the season. Or, you might do the change-out between Thanksgiving and New Year, when food banks are especially in need. Supplies go to a good cause; you can take a tax write-off; you won't worry about things freezing in your unheated summer cottage or rats ransacking your boat after it's laid up.
4. Order a complete program of X calories for Y days from survival food providers (see Appendix for suggestions). These companies offer neatly packaged food plans, usually consisting of dehydrated fruit and vegetables, soy meat substitutes, whole wheat, and dry milk. Stow them away, discard and replace them as they expire, or donate before they do, and thank heaven you never had to eat the stuff.

An easy, fun way to rotate supplies is to throw a big party, picnic, or reunion and use recipes from this book.

Per Person, Per Day
Rule of Thumb

1 or 2 eggs

1 cup flour or other milled grain for
   recipes

2 cups whole grains

1 cup (or more) milk for drinking
   and recipes

½ cup vegetable oil, butter or other
   fats

1 to 2 cups fruit

2 cups vegetables

1 cup (8 ounces) meat, seafood,
   poultry, egg, or meat substitute

1 gallon water for drinking and
   cooking

With this starting point, decide what items on your list will be fresh, canned, frozen, dehydrated, freeze-dried, and so on depending on your own lifestyle. Then add spices and condiments to suit to your style.

Lazy Cook's Shopping List

Make a menu for a week's meals for the number of people you will be feeding. Then create a shopping list to go with it and simply multiply it by the number of weeks you are preparing for. If you want to be prepared for a longer period, make a two-week list and it's a good bet nobody will realize you're having pancakes every other Sunday morning and ham and beans every other Saturday night. The menu doesn't have to be rigid and repetitive. If your menu calls for canned seafood every Tuesday for

When you're planning for a set length of time, stock one extra day's supplies for each day you will be away.

dinner or griddle cakes for Sunday breakfast there are countless variations on the basic theme.

How It Might Work

There is no easy way for someone else to outline a meal plan that will work for you and your family, using foods in your pantry, under all conditions. One point of this book is the advantage of stocking an ample, balanced pantry so you'll have choices depending on the nature of the need.

We all have special likes and dietary needs and no-no's as well as different cooking styles and facilities. One of the readers of my Camp and RV Cook blog, (http://www.campandrvcook.blogspot.com/), is a 20-something man traveling alone in a van. He carries little more than canned ravioli and spaghetti, which suits him just fine. A follower of my Boat Cook blog (http://www.boatcook.blogspot.com/) lives on Triscuits, almond butter, and dried apricots. She couldn't care less about cooking.

Many of us today must provision for regular diets as well as for a person who is vegan, diabetic, or managing celiac disease. In everyday life most of us literally depend on our daily bread. In emergencies, however, daily baking becomes difficult. Other starches, such as rice, must fill out a menu.

Some emergencies may require you to have your main meal early in the day, even if it isn't your usual habit, to make use of daylight during a blackout or when requiring sun for a solar oven.

14-Day Meal Plan, Per Person

Breakfast

14 portions oatmeal, other hot cereal, muesli, eggs with biscuit or bread, pancakes

14 portions fruit or juice

Beverages, including milk, to use on hot cereals and in making pancake batter

Lunch or Supper

14 portions, two cups each, soup or salad

14 portions bread, crackers, or biscuits

14 servings, ½ cup each, fruit

14 servings dessert or a simple sweet, such as hard candy

14 pints beverage

Dinner

14 servings (4 ounces) meat, fish, egg, or protein substitute

14 portions (½ cup each) starch such as potato, rice, pasta

Additional starch for heavy eaters (might be bread, tortilla, biscuit)

28 portions green and yellow vegetables, ⅓ to ½ cup each, served hot, as salad, or as an ingredient in a one-dish meal

14 servings dessert

14 pints beverage

A good supply of bread sticks or corn sticks is a great meal stretcher for any meal of the day.

Extra Meal, such as Elevenses, Tea, Midnight Snack
7 cups nuts, dried fruit, or a mixture (½ cup per person per day) AND/OR 14 to 28 cups (popped) popcorn (one to two cups per person per day) AND/OR crackers, nut butter
14 pints beverage

Other needs
Condiments
Spreads such as peanut butter
Oils for cooking and salad dressing
Cream and sugar for coffee

Practice Makes Perfect

By using pantry recipes regularly you are not only rotating supplies, you're rehearsing for the time when they may be the only foods on hand. Make notes in this book. What did your family like? What did you learn to do or not do? If you ran out of this or that, what substitutes worked in the recipe? What pantry supplies will you increase and decrease on your next shopping trip?

It's Crucial to Read Labels

Around the world, government rules about labeling keep changing. As they change, so does the information listed on food labels. For example, they may or may not indicate whether the product is GMO or has been subjected to peanut or wheat exposure. As you shop for pantry foods, pay attention to important basic label statistics.

Manufacturer Information: Some codes on cans and packages aren't meant to be read by consumers. They refer to the date an item was canned or the batch number of the product. These numbers come in handy if there is a recall and, if you call the company to complain about a product, you'll need them.

Nutrition Facts: A typical paper label starts with data that lists the serving size and number of servings per can or package. Red alert! Serving size is often minuscule compared to what you'll actually consume. This deception is almost universal in snacks and sweets sold as "healthier" or "lower in fat," but it also applies to almost every food on the shelf.

Most of us don't pay much attention to nutrition facts, but they're important if you're diabetic, allergic, or a carb counter, or are concerned with specifics such as sodium or fat content. Serving size is very important to everyone, but it's also the most likely item on the label to be overlooked. I once prepared a 10-serving can of a popular freeze-dried entrée sold to campers and preppers. It served four. Dividing it into 10 servings would have made for a very skimpy meal. Yet by eating larger servings everyone was getting 2½ times the sodium, fat, and carbs listed as being in one serving.

Only by reading labels can you assure that you're getting the best nutrition per dollar, per ounce, per portion, and per cubic foot of storage space.

It's essential to read labels and know just how much food you're getting per ounce, per dollar, and per cubic inch.

Chapter 4

Bracing Breakfasts

Whether you are preparing for a fun activity or are experiencing an emergency, breakfast sets the tempo for the rest of the day. It's also the meal where most of us expect traditional comfort foods from childhood: biscuits and sausage gravy, steel-cut oatmeal with butter and brown sugar, a full English breakfast with kippers and broiled tomatoes, beans and toast, sticky rice and miso soup, or perhaps just a steaming cup of tea or coffee. When these comforts aren't available it's important to have substitutes to energize and appeal.

One of the toughest assignments is to make toast, a breakfast favorite in western cuisine. You may have neither fresh bread nor an electric toaster. This chapter focuses on other forms of hearty carbs to jump-start the day. These recipes don't stray far from traditional breakfast fare, yet they're made from pantry provisions.

BUTTERSCOTCH PUNCH

MAKES 6 CUPS

Here's one way to make a hot breakfast drink from your pantry shelf.

> ¾ cup brown sugar, packed
>
> 1 cup water
>
> 2 cups nonfat dry milk
>
> 1 teaspoon vanilla extract or butter-rum flavoring
>
> Pinch salt
>
> 5 cups water

Stir brown sugar and the cup of water with the milk powder in a cold saucepan. Then cook over low heat, stirring to dissolve sugar. Gradually stir in flavorings and salt. Reduce heat, stir in 5 cups water, and heat until steamy. Makes 6 cups. Caution: milk scorches easily. Keep the flame low and be patient.

MOCHA COCOA MIX

MAKES 7 cups OF MIX (55 CUPS OF COCOA)

Save money and create your own mixes. You can also customize contents by using, say, a sugar substitute or your favorite brand of cocoa.

> 1 cup brown sugar
>
> 1 cup white sugar
>
> 2 cups dry milk
>
> 2 cups powdered creamer, regular or French vanilla
>
> 1 cup unsweetened cocoa
>
> ½ cup instant coffee granules

Mix well and keep cool and dry. Put 2 tablespoons mix in a mug and fill halfway with boiling water. Stir well then fill the cup with more boiling water. Depending on the size of your mugs you may need more or less of the dry mix. Store mix in a cool, dry place.

SUNSHINE RICE

Tortillas are available in many packages, including some found on the supermarket shelf. Individually packaged, long-life tortillas made to government MRE specifications are available online in case lots.

> 2 tablespoons olive oil
>
> 3 cups cooked rice
>
> 15-ounce can carrots, drained and finely chopped
>
> Orange marmalade
>
> 2 tablespoons sugar
>
> 6 eggs or equivalent
>
> Small can evaporated milk (⅔ cup)
>
> Tortillas

Spread olive oil in a large skillet. Spread rice in an even layer and sprinkle with carrots. In a bowl whisk 1 tablespoon orange marmalade, sugar, eggs, and milk. Pour over skillet. Cover and cook over low-medium heat until set. Serve as is or spoon into tortillas spread with orange marmalade.

BRANOLA

MAKES 8 half cups

> 1 cup wheat or rice bran
>
> 2 cups rolled oats (minute or old-fashioned)
>
> 1 cup dried fruit and chopped nuts
>
> 1 tablespoon apple pie spice or plain cinnamon
>
> ½ cup honey
>
> 3 tablespoons coconut oil

Set the oven to 350°F. Spray a large baking pan or two smaller pans. Place bran, oats, nuts, fruit, and spice in a large bag and shake gently to mix. Empty bag into pan(s) and drizzle with honey and coconut oil. Bake 5 minutes, stir, and bake 3 to 5 minutes more. Cool completely and keep cool and dry.

Branola makes a satisfying snack or breakfast. Add fresh fruit to the dried if you have some on hand. (Public Domain)

SALTINE SKILLET OMELET

SERVES 2

No bread? No toaster? No problem, with this hearty, one-dish omelet.

> 12 saltine crackers
>
> ½ teaspoon pepper
>
> 1 tablespoon vegetable oil
>
> 4 eggs or equivalent reconstituted eggs
>
> Small can (⅔ cup) evaporated milk
>
> *Optional extras:* bacon bits, canned ham, chopped onion, green
>   pepper, grated cheese
>
> Worcestershire sauce

Put the saltines and pepper in a freezer bag and squeeze to coarsely crush crackers. Spread oil evenly around bottom and sides of a cold, nonstick skillet. Add the crackers. Add eggs and milk to the bag and squeeze to mix well. Pour egg mixture into the skillet and scatter with any extras you choose to add. Cover the skillet and cook over medium-low heat until eggs set. Pass the Worcestershire sauce.

RAMEN OMELET FOR TWO

SERVES 2

Use ramen with or without the flavoring packet and customize the recipe to your own breakfast tastes. Although they are bulky, noodles that "cook" in their own container are a convenient starch course.

> 1 packet ramen
>
> Hot water
>
> 3 or 4 eggs or equivalent
>
> 1 tablespoon vegetable oil
>
> Seasonings to taste

Add hot water to the tub according to package directions. While noodles steep, heat oil in a nonstick skillet. Drain ramen and spread in the skillet. Add eggs. Cover and cook over low heat until eggs set.

SCRAMBLED MATZOH

SERVES 2–3

Not just for Passover any more, matzoh is available in supermarkets year-round. Add it to your list of shelf-stable breads. Keep it cool and dry and watch use-by dates. This tangy recipe is easily doubled or quadrupled to feed a larger crew.

> 2 whole matzoh, broken up
>
> Water
>
> Small can evaporated milk
>
> 1 tablespoon horseradish (optional)
>
> 4 to 6 eggs or equivalent in reconstituted eggs
>
> 3 tablespoons canola oil
>
> ½ cup shredded dry cheese such as Parmesan (optional)
>
> 15-ounce can diced tomatoes, drained

Put matzoh in a plastic bag and cover with water. Let soak. In a bowl whisk milk, horseradish, and eggs. Use an ice pick to punch holes in the plastic bag, drain it and squeeze matzoh dry. Fold matzoh into eggs. Heat oil in a nonstick skillet and spread egg mixture in an even layer. Top with half the cheese, tomatoes, and remaining cheese. Cover and cook over medium heat until eggs set.

Hot to Go

Wake up to hot oatmeal for two. Preheat a one-quart, stainless steel, wide-mouth thermos bottle with hot water. Discard that water and add 2 cups boiling water and 1 cup old-fashioned or minute oats (not steel cut). Seal the thermos and tip gently to mix. In the morning spoon out hot, creamy oatmeal. Makes two servings of one cup each.

RICE WEDGIES

SERVES 3–4

Fully cooked rice comes in shelf-stable pouches. You might also try using a different, cooked-from-scratch rice each time. There are 40,000 varieties of rice worldwide!

> 3 eggs or equivalent
>
> ⅓ cup water
>
> ½ teaspoon each salt, celery seed, pepper
>
> 1 tablespoon powdered coffee creamer
>
> 3 cups cooked rice
>
> Half of a 16-ounce package of process cheese, diced
>
> 4-ounce can diced green chilies, well drained
>
> 2-ounce jar diced pimentos, well drained

Grease or spray a 10-inch skillet. Put eggs, water, seasonings, and creamer in a plastic bag and squeeze bag to mix well. Add rice, cheese, chilies, and pimentos and squeeze bag to mix. Turn the mixture into the skillet, cover, and cook over low-medium heat until it's set, firm, and lightly browned around edges. Flip it out on a cutting board and cut in wedges.

SUNRISE SAUSAGE GRAVY

SERVES 6–8

Canned sausage is available online and in supermarkets. Sausage flavor TVP is available in health food stores and from survival food suppliers.

> 1½ cups cooked, crumbled sausage or equivalent
>
> 16-ounce package shelf-stable process cheese (such as Velveeta)
>
> ⅓ cup water
>
> 1 tablespoon flour or cornstarch
>
> ⅓ cup water
>
> 12-ounce can evaporated milk
>
> Hot sauce to taste
>
> Freshly ground pepper

Put sausage, diced cheese, and ⅓ cup water in a heavy saucepan over low heat. Stir until cheese melts. Stir flour or cornstarch into ⅓ cup cold water and stir into the sausage mixture. Heat, stirring until mixture thickens. Stir in evaporated milk and heat gently but do not boil. Serve over biscuits, grits, porridge, polenta, etc.

TOMATO SOUP COFFEE CAKE

SERVES 9

Let your family guess what's in this spicy, low-fat cake. The tomato soup adds nutrition and serves as a shortcut ingredient to replace shortening.

> ½ cup sugar
>
> 1 egg or equivalent
>
> 1 tablespoon vegetable oil
>
> 1 teaspoon each cinnamon, nutmeg
>
> 1 can condensed tomato soup
>
> 1 teaspoon baking soda
>
> 1½ cups flour
>
> 8-ounce jar maraschino cherries, cut up
>
> ½ cup chopped nuts (optional)

In a bowl whisk together sugar, egg, oil, spices, and soup. Stir in the baking soda and flour until everything is evenly moistened. Drain cherries, saving the juice. Fold cherries and nuts into the batter. Bake in an 8-inch square pan 30 to 35 minutes or until springy at 350°F. Use the round handle of a wooden spoon to make several holes in the cake and drizzle the cherry juice into them. Serves up to 9 as a breakfast side dish.

GLAZED HAM PANCAKES

SERVES 2

This makes a hearty breakfast, lunch, or dinner for two. It's easily stretched to make more servings by using more batter with the same or larger can of ham.

> 1 cup flour
>
> 1 teaspoon baking powder
>
> ¼ teaspoon baking soda
>
> Liquid
>
> 1 teaspoon prepared mustard
>
> 5- to 7-ounce can chunk ham

Glaze

> ½ cup brown sugar
>
> ¼ cup prepared mustard
>
> ¼ cup water
>
> Pancake syrup (optional)

In a medium bowl whisk flour, baking powder, and baking soda. Add mustard, liquid from ham, and enough water or milk to make a medium batter. While ham is still in the can, twist a fork in it to break it up, then fold into batter. Fry as for pancakes.

To make glaze stir mustard, sugar, and water until smooth and spread a little on each pancake. Serve as is or with syrup.

BLUE BREAKFAST

SERVES 3–4

> 16-ounce can Boston brown bread, sliced ½ inch thick
>
> 1 jar of Roka blue cheese spread OR about ⅔ cup reconstituted dried blue cheese
>
> 1 can of pears in their own juice

Spread half the bread slices with blue cheese. Drain pears well and save the juice to make a breakfast fruit punch. Slice pears thinly and place atop cheese-spread bread slices. Top with another slice of bread. Makes 5 to 6 sandwiches to serve 3 to 4.

BUTTERSCOTCH BREAKFAST BOWL

SERVES 4–5

> 2 eggs
>
> 3½ cups milk
>
> 1 cup dark brown sugar
>
> 2 cups one-minute oats (not instant, old-fashioned, or steel cut)
>
> ¼ cup peanut butter

In a cold saucepan, whisk eggs and milk. Stir in sugar and oats. Cook, stirring over low-medium heat until thickened. Stir in peanut butter. Cover, remove from heat, and let stand 3 to 5 minutes. Serve in cereal bowls as is or with milk, cream, jelly, or more peanut butter.

BREAKFAST PINE CONES

Nuts and seeds are a good source of healthful fats, but they can get rancid. Watch use-by dates and keep cool.

> Rye Crisp crackers, 2 per person
>
> Peanut butter (creamy is best for easier spreading)
>
> Orange-flavored dry gelatin dessert mix, regular or sugar-free
>
> Sunflower nuts or pine nuts

"Butter" crackers with peanut butter and sprinkle very lightly with dry gelatin dessert mix. (For a small batch you may not need the entire package.) Fill a plate with nuts and press gently with the peanut butter side of the cracker so it picks up a coating of nuts.

BRITISH BEANS FOR BREAKFAST

SERVES 5–8

Canned baked beans are served over toast in British breakfasts, and the tradition is also followed in many former British colonies. Simply open a can or make this tastier version.

> 20-ounce can of white beans such as navy beans or Great Northerns OR 2½ cups cooked white beans
>
> 8-ounce tin tomato sauce
>
> 1 teaspoon browning concentrate such as Gravy Master or Bovril
>
> ¼ cup molasses or dark brown sugar
>
> ½ teaspoon each crumbled, dried sage, thyme, ground cinnamon
>
> 2 tablespoons Barbados rum (optional)
>
> 2 tablespoons Worcestershire sauce

Heat everything together, adjust seasonings and serve over toast or a substitute.

BREAKFAST FRY

SERVES 4–6

This recipe works best in cooler weather or when the dish can be refrigerated. You'll also need two pans the same size. Longer pastas and noodles bind together best to make the solid brick called for here.

> 3 to 4 cups hot, cooked, and drained spaghetti, fettuccine, or noodles
>
> 2 eggs or equivalent egg substitute
>
> Flour
>
> Salt, pepper
>
> Herb or spice*
>
> Oil for frying
>
> Choice of topping

Line a 9 x 13-inch pan with plastic wrap, overhanging a few inches. Spray wrap with nonstick coating. Spread warm pasta or noodles in an even layer and cover with plastic wrap. Put a second 9 x 13-inch pan on top and weigh it down with a stone or some canned goods. Cool or chill overnight.

Lift out the now-solid pasta or noodle "brick" and cut in squares. Dip in beaten egg, then in seasoned flour. Fry in hot oil until crusty. Serve slathered in hot applesauce, sausage gravy, stewed fruit, cheese sauce, or what have you.

You might use a little cinnamon if you'll cover the fries with applesauce, or a pinch of thyme if serving the fries with sausage gravy.

Chapter 5
Makeshift Main Dishes

One-dish meals are always a plus when you're short of time, fuel, water, or other resources. Made from pantry staples, these easy dishes will please both belly and budget. Most can be made with a campfire, grill, or camp stove.

Main Dishes with Meat

In my family, we home-can meat just as routinely as peaches or tomatoes. It was always a special treat for us kids to come home from a fun day at the beach or mall to a quick dinner that Mother threw together by combining home-canned chicken with rice and vegetables. No thawing nor long cook times were required. Mother's canned chicken was associated with good times.

Later as a camper and sailor, I rediscovered the convenience of home-canned meats. I preserve only boneless, well-trimmed meat with no salt or chemicals. A pressure cooker makes canning quick and safe. Jars and rings are reusable, so the only cost is for canning lids. When cruising without refrigeration, empty jars come in handy to can fish when the catch is too large to consume in one day.

These recipes call for commercially canned meats. If you home-can meat it's easy to remember that "a pint's a pound." A general rule of thumb is to allow four ounces of meat per serving.

FEAST DAY HAM

SERVES 6–8

When the calendar calls for a holiday, bring out the canned ham you put away for just such an occasion.

> 2-pound canned ham
>
> ¼ teaspoon ground cloves
>
> 15-ounce can whole cranberry sauce
>
> ⅓ cup honey
>
> ⅓ cup water
>
> ¼ cup dried onion bits

Heat ham by whatever means you have. In a saucepan mash cranberry sauce with honey, cloves, water, and onions. Heat gently, stirring until cranberry sauce melts and onions soften. Slice ham and serve with sauce.

CORNED BEEFCAKES

SERVES 6

> 6 servings of instant mashed potato flakes
>
> ¼ cup diced dried onion bits
>
> Water
>
> 12-ounce can corned beef
>
> Large egg or equivalent
>
> Flour
>
> Freshly ground pepper
>
> Vegetable oil for frying
>
> Ketchup (optional)

Put potato flakes and onion in a bowl and add enough hot water to moisten. Let stand a few minutes and add more water if needed. Stir in corned beef, breaking it up with a fork, until evenly mixed. Stir in egg. Spread a little flour on a plate and shower lightly with freshly ground pepper. Heat a thin layer of oil in a large skillet. Make six patties with the beef and potato mixture. Dip patties lightly in flour and fry until crusty on both sides. Pass the ketchup.

HAM SHORTCAKE

SERVES 6

Cornbread is suggested here, but the ham mixture can also be served over biscuits, rice, rice cakes, potatoes, or other starch.

> 6 servings of cornbread (your own recipe or from a box)
>
> 1 pound canned ham, diced, or equivalent in reconstituted ham dices
>
> 4 cups water
>
> 1⅔ cups nonfat dry milk
>
> ½ cup flour
>
> 2 tablespoons each dried onion flakes, celery flakes, sweet pepper flakes
>
> 1 teaspoon dry mustard
>
> 2 tablespoons real bacon bits (optional)
>
> ½ cup chopped peanuts

In a cold saucepan whisk together dry milk, flour, flakes, and dry mustard. Gradually whisk in water. Bring milk mixture to a low boil over medium-low heat, stirring until it thickens. Fold in ham to heat through. Spoon over cornbread and sprinkle with bacon bits and/or chopped peanuts.

CHICKEN-IN-A-BLANKET

SERVES 8–10

It's easy to whip up this recipe in the small galley, and potluck guests love the creamy mixture with its buttery topping.

2 or 3 cans, 10 ounces each, chunk chicken

15-ounce can sliced carrots, drained

15-ounce can sliced green beans, drained

Water

1 can condensed cream of chicken soup

2 tablespoons cornstarch

2 cups self-rising flour

½ teaspoon baking soda

1 stick butter or butter-flavored shortening, melted

1½ cups milk, soured with 2 teaspoons vinegar

Set the oven for 400°F and grease a 9 x 13-inch casserole. Drain chicken and vegetables into a 2-cup measure and add water to make 1½ cups liquid. Arrange drained chicken and vegetables in casserole. In a bowl whisk together liquid, soup, and cornstarch. Pour evenly over chicken mixture. Dry the bowl with paper towels and whisk together self-rising flour, soda, melted butter, and sour milk. Pour batter oven chicken mixture. Bake about 40 minutes or until a golden crust forms on top. Makes 8 to 10 potluck portions.

Stovetop method: Using a large, heavy, deep, cold skillet, proceed as above. Cover and place over a low burner and cook without peeking 25 minutes, then cover and cook (uncovering as little as possible) until filling is thickened and creamy topping is springy to the touch. Topping may not get brown.

Campfire method: Grease a Dutch oven and proceed as above. Cover and place oven in well-started coals, piling them up sides and on top. After 25 minutes check for doneness. Topping may not get brown, but it helps to have a flat lid for the Dutch oven and keep it heaped with hot coals.

BRUNSWICK STEW

SERVES 20

The classic, Low Country way to make this stew in the old days required a huge kettle, stirring all day with wood paddles until the meat fell from the bones of squirrels, rabbits, wild boar, birds, venison, and whatever other beasts were brought in from the day's hunt. Traditionally it should contain at least three meats.

Here is a shortcut version. Amounts include juices from all canned goods except the onions. It's a great party or potluck dish and a good way to rotate a large stock of canned foods.

> 3 cans, 10 to 12 ounces each, chunk chicken
>
> 3 cans, 10 to 12 ounces each, roast beef, cut up
>
> 2 cans, 10 to 12 ounces each, chunk turkey
>
> 1 can, 10 to 12 ounces, chunk ham
>
> 2 cans, 32 ounces each, diced tomatoes
>
> 2 jars small, whole boiled onions (also called Holland onions), drained
>
> ½ cup Worcestershire sauce
>
> 16-ounce bottle ketchup
>
> 10-ounce jar chili sauce or mild salsa
>
> 1 tablespoon dry mustard
>
> ½ stick butter or butter flavor shortening (optional) OR ½ cup lard (optional)
>
> 2 cans, 15 ounces each, small lima beans
>
> 2 cans, 15 ounces each, cream-style corn
>
> 2 cans, 15 ounces each, diced potatoes
>
> Salt and pepper to taste
>
> Hot sauce

Put the canned meat in a large kettle or cauldron, breaking it up as you go. Add the tomatoes, onions, Worcestershire, ketchup, salsa, and mustard. Stir well. Bring to a boil over high heat, stirring occasionally. Cover, reduce heat, and cook 20 to 30 minutes. Add the butter or lard, limas, corn, and potatoes. Cover and simmer over low flame, stirring occasionally until heated through. Taste and add salt and pepper if needed. Ladle into soup bowls. Pass the hot sauce.

LUCKY NEW YEAR BLACK-EYED PEAS

SERVES 4

In the Dixie states, eating hog jowls (rhymes with bowls) and black-eyed peas on New Year's Eve or New Year's Day is thought to bring good luck in the coming year. Eat them any time. Black-eyed peas are available dried, canned, fresh, or frozen. Ham is also available in many forms.

  2 cups dried black-eyed peas OR 4 or 5 cups ready-to-eat black-eyed peas

  10-ounce can chunk ham

  4 tablespoons dried onion bits

  1 teaspoon dried granular garlic

  1 tablespoon parsley flakes

  1 teaspoon vinegar (optional)

  1 bay leaf

  1 or 2 drops smoke flavoring (optional)

  Tabasco

Cook peas according to package directions. Break up ham and mix all ingredients. Heat through. Discard bay leaf and serve as is or over rice. Serves 4 or more depending on rice supply. Pass the Tabasco.

CHICKENACHO CASSEROLE

SERVES 4–6

Use drained canned chicken or reconstituted chicken bites. Tortillas can be homemade, from the supermarket shelf, or long-life tortillas from specialty suppliers.

> 3 to 4 cups cooked, bite-size chicken pieces
>
> 2 to 3 cups torn corn tortillas
>
> 1 can condensed cream of onion soup
>
> 1 can Rotel tomatoes (mild, medium, or hot)
>
> 10-ounce jar cheese spread such as Cheez-Whiz

Spray a large, nonstick skillet. Scatter chicken bits in the bottom and top with torn tortillas. Spoon by spoon, distribute soup, tomatoes, and cheese evenly over the top. Cover tightly and cook over low flame until everything is heated through.

RISI E BISI

SERVES 4–6

When subjected to the canning process, peas get mushy and lose their bright green color. This is one dish where it pays to use reconstituted freeze-dried peas.

> 3 tablespoons diced dried onion bits
>
> ¼ cup white wine, broth, water, or juice from canned ham
>
> 2 tablespoons olive oil
>
> 2 cups short-grain or arborio rice
>
> ½ teaspoon garlic powder
>
> 10-ounce can chunk ham
>
> 4 cups water
>
> 4 teaspoons chicken base or powdered bouillon
>
> 2 cups prepared freeze-dried peas

Soak dried onions in liquid 15 minutes or more. Heat olive oil and sauté raw rice, gradually stirring in onion and ham. Add water, garlic powder, and chicken base. Bring to a boil, cover, and simmer over low heat until rice is tender and water is absorbed. Stir in prepared peas and heat gently until they're tender. Serve at once.

SHORTCUT CINCINNATI CHILI

SERVES 6

> 2 cans roast beef in gravy
>
> 12-ounce can or jar small onions (aka Holland onions)
>
> 1 teaspoon cinnamon
>
> 1 tablespoon flour or cornstarch
>
> ¼ teaspoon each cloves, ground ginger
>
> 10-ounce can sliced mushrooms, drained
>
> 15-ounce can kidney beans, undrained
>
> Cooked spaghetti

Open the canned beef and use clean scissors to snip through it, breaking it up in the can. Drain onions, cut them in half and drain cut side down. In a one-cup measure mix flour or cornstarch and spices. Add cold water to make a paste, then stir in some of the beef gravy. Add water to make one cup.

Over medium heat, stir liquid until it begins to thicken. Empty cans of beef into the pot. Stir in onions, kidney beans, and mushrooms and heat through. Serve over a starch.

Cook's note: Authentic Cincinnati "chili" is served over spaghetti but any starch base would be good here.

Solving the "Serve-Over" Problem

One of the biggest bugaboos for the cook who has only one pot or one burner is "one-dish" recipes that end with "serve over noodles" or "spoon over rice." What you expected to be a one-pot dish then requires a starch base cooked separately. Here are "serve over" solutions that don't require a separate pan or burner.

Biscuits, bread, toast, Melba toast

Crisp Chinese noodles

Croutons

Crumbled crackers or matzo

Drained, French-cut green beans

Fresh sprouts

Coarsely grated vegetable such as cabbage

Polenta

Potato sticks

Pre-cooked pouch foods such as rice

Pre-baked pastry shells

Refried beans from a can or pouch

Rice cakes

Rye crispbread

Tortillas

Zwieback or rusk

By adding very hot water you can also create these "serve over" solutions in a bowl:

Instant grits, mashed potatoes

Stuffing mix

Ramen

FAVA BEAN 'N BACON STEW

SERVES 4

Fava beans, also called broad beans, are a nutritional powerhouse. They're available fresh, canned, or dried. These supersize beans have tough skins that most people prefer to remove. Just squeeze them one-by-one and let the meaty center pop out. In this recipe use canned favas or prepare dried beans according to package directions.

> 2 tablespoons vegetable oil
>
> 3-ounce package or jar real bacon bits
>
> ¼ cup flour
>
> 2 cups water
>
> 1 tablespoon granular garlic
>
> 4 cups cooked fava beans, skins removed if you wish
>
> Salt and pepper to taste

Heat oil and stir in a teaspoon of the bacon until fragrant. Whisk flour into cold water, then stir into oil mixture with the garlic until thick and bubbly. Stir in beans to heat through. Season to taste. Sprinkle with remaining bacon bits.

LAZY DAY BEAN GRAVY

Select a gravy mix that calls for two cups of milk or water or use two smaller packages.

> 1 packet sausage gravy mix
>
> 2 cups milk or water
>
> 1 can baked beans
>
> Seasonings to taste

Prepare the gravy mix according to package directions. When it thickens, stir in beans to heat through. Season to taste. This is good over potatoes, rice, noodles, biscuits, or what have you.

GINGER PEACHY CHICKEN

SERVES 4–6

To avoid excess sweetness, buy peaches canned in their own juice, not syrup.

> 2 cans, 10 ounces each, chunk breast of chicken
>
> 1 tablespoon vegetable oil
>
> 1 tablespoon cornstarch
>
> ½ teaspoon ground ginger
>
> 15-ounce can of peaches, coarsely chopped
>
> ½ cup juice from the peaches
>
> Heaping tablespoon peanut butter
>
> 1 cup lightly salted peanuts, chopped (optional) OR 1 cup crumbled ginger snaps (optional)

Drain chicken well, saving broth in a small bowl or cup. Heat oil in a skillet or saucepan and brown chicken. Stir cornstarch, ginger, and a few spoons of peach juice into the broth, followed by the remaining peach juice and peanut butter. Add broth mixture to the chicken, stirring over gentle heat, until the sauce thickens. Spoon over rice, noodles, mashed potatoes, or what have you. Sprinkle with peanuts or crumbled ginger snaps.

CHICKEN ALMOND CURRY

SERVES 6

> 2 tablespoons vegetable oil
>
> 4 tablespoons dried onion bits
>
> 1 teaspoon celery seed
>
> 1 tablespoon curry powder
>
> 1½ cups raw rice
>
> 4 cups water
>
> 4 chicken bouillon cubes
>
> 1 cup golden raisins

> 6 servings freeze-dried diced chicken, reconstituted, OR 2 cans, 10 ounces each, canned breast of chicken
>
> About ½ cup slivered or sliced almonds

Heat oil and stir in onion bits, celery seed, curry powder, and rice until fragrant. Add water, bouillon, raisins, and chicken. Bring to a boil. Cover, reduce heat, and cook 20 minutes or until rice is tender. Sprinkle each portion with almonds.

CHICKEN CASBAH

SERVES 4–6

> 2 cups boneless, skinless bites of canned or reconstituted chicken
>
> ¼ cup dried onion bits
>
> 1 teaspoon dried parsley
>
> 1 teaspoon each ground ginger, cinnamon
>
> ¼ teaspoon garlic granules
>
> 2 cups water (including any juice from the chicken)
>
> 8 pitted dried plums
>
> ¼ cup honey
>
> ½ cup sliced almonds or broken cashews (optional)
>
> 1 tablespoon vegetable oil
>
> 1 or 2 cans garbanzo beans (chickpeas), drained and rinsed

Drain canned chicken and use the juice as part of the water measurement. Twist a fork in the can to break up chicken. Combine everything but the nuts, oil, and chickpeas in a saucepan or pressure cooker. Bring to a boil and cook 2 minutes under pressure or 20 minutes at a low simmer. In a small, nonstick skillet cook nuts in hot oil until golden brown. Fold chickpeas into the chicken mixture. Heat through. Sprinkle each portion with toasted nuts.

MEXICAN MEATBALL STEW

SERVES 4–6

Canned meat won't solidify in cooking as raw meat does for making meatloaf or meatballs. Raw eggs are added to "set" the meatballs; they also add protein.

> 15-ounce can roast beef hash
>
> 2 eggs or equivalent in reconstituted powdered eggs
>
> 1 tablespoon flour
>
> 28-ounce can of diced tomatoes and their juice
>
> 2 cups water
>
> Small can chopped green chilies, drained
>
> 2 tablespoons dried onion bits
>
> 1 teaspoon each garlic powder, dried oregano, sugar
>
> 2 teaspoons chili powder
>
> 1 to 2 cups cooked rice
>
> Freshly ground pepper to taste
>
> Hot sauce

In a bowl mash hash thoroughly with the eggs and flour. Set aside. In a saucepan mix tomatoes, water, chilies, dried onion, sugar, and herbs. Bring to a low boil. Using two teaspoons, drop blobs of hash mixture into the actively simmering soup. Work slowly to keep soup simmering and don't crowd or rush the meatballs as they firm up. When meatballs are cooked, gently stir in rice and heat through. Pass the pepper grinder and hot sauce.

FRIED CORN SKILLET

SERVES 4–6

Corn is one of the most versatile foods in the pantry, so useful it can become boring. Frying is one way to add interesting new taste and texture. The secret is to use a hot skillet and to keep frying until the corn and Spam or tofu are flecked with toasty brown bits.

> 2 tablespoons vegetable oil
>
> ½ teaspoon curry powder
>
> 12-ounce can of low-sodium Spam, diced, OR
> > 12-ounce brick of extra-firm tofu, diced
>
> 10- to 12-ounce can of whole kernel corn with green and
> > red pepper
>
> 10-ounce can of white shoepeg corn
>
> 15-ounce can of whole kernel corn
>
> 1 teaspoon dried, crumbled thyme, basil, parsley, or herb of choice
>
> Salt and pepper to taste

Heat the oil in a large skillet and sizzle Spam or tofu with curry powder. Drain corn and gradually stir it into the skillet over high heat. Keep stir-frying to bring up browned bits from the bottom of the skillet. When every-thing is toasty, fold in your herb of choice. Adjust seasonings and serve.

For a creamier dish, stir in tinned cream to taste just before serving. Heat, but do not boil.

SPAM "STEAK" FOR SINGLES

Fortunately for singles, more and more foods are now available in small portions in a can or pouch.

> Single slice packet of Spam
>
> 1 teaspoon dried onion bits
>
> 1 teaspoon vegetable oil
>
> Small can sweet potatoes (preferably packed in water, not syrup)
>
> 4 dried apricots, snipped into quarters

Drain Spam into a small container and soak onion bits. In a nonstick skillet, sizzle the whole Spam slice in hot oil until it's browned. Add onion, sweet potatoes and their juice, and apricots. Cover and cook over very low heat until everything is heated through.

Variation: Soak snipped apricots for an hour first in a little rum or apricot liqueur.

ONE POT TAMALES

SERVES 4–6

With apologies to cooks who make real tamales in corn husks, here's a recipe that cooks in a single pot.

> 4 portions meat, chicken, or meat substitute
>
> 1 teaspoon garlic granules
>
> 1 tablespoon each dried green pepper, diced onion bits
>
> 15-ounce can diced tomatoes
>
> 15-ounce can whole kernel corn
>
> 2 teaspoons chili powder
>
> 1 cup cold water*
>
> ½ cup yellow cornmeal
>
> Small can sliced black olives, drained

Put meat in a saucepan with the garlic, green pepper, onion, tomatoes, and corn. Stir in chili powder. Heat to a low boil. Stir cornmeal into cold water then blend into the meat mixture. Cook over low-medium heat, stirring until thickened. Add in black olives and serve. Spoon onto serving plates. Pass the pepper mill.

* Use liquid drained from the corn as part of the water measure.

Main Dishes with Seafood off the Shelf

SEAFOOD POLENTA

SERVES 4

This recipe stretches your supply of whatever seafood you have on hand, from fresh-caught to canned or reconstituted. Use one type of seafood or a mixture such as canned shrimp, crab, and clams.

> 1 cup yellow cornmeal
>
> 1 teaspoon salt
>
> 1 teaspoon dried Italian seasoning
>
> 1 cup cold water*
>
> 3 cups boiling water
>
> 2 tablespoons dried diced onion
>
> 2 tablespoons olive oil
>
> Small can sliced mushrooms, drained
>
> 1½ cups seafood in bite size
>
> Grated Parmesan cheese
>
> *Optional: Use liquid drained from canned seafood as part of the water measure. Omit salt.

Combine cornmeal, salt, seasoning, and cold water. In a saucepan bring 3 cups water to a boil and stir in cornmeal mixture with onion and olive oil. Cook, stirring, about 15 minutes or until cornmeal is thick and creamy. Fold in mushrooms and seafood and spoon onto serving plates. Sprinkle with Parmesan.

Cook's note: This can also be made with salt fish that has been soaked and desalted according to package directions. Omit salt from cornmeal mixture.

SALMON APPLE SKILLET

SERVES 4

    1 can condensed cream of celery soup

    ½ teaspoon each dried dillweed, dried thyme, celery seed

    2 cans, 15 or 16 ounces each, red or pink salmon

    1 tablespoon vegetable oil

    15-ounce can pie-sliced apples in water, undrained

    15-ounce can small potatoes, drained and cut up

    Optional topping:

        ½ cup dry bread crumbs

        2 tablespoons vegetable oil

Drain salmon and discard skin and bones if you wish. Spread the condensed soup in a large, sprayed skillet. Sprinkle with herbs. Top with chunks of salmon, apples, and potatoes. Cover and cook over low heat until everything is heated through. Stir and serve. Sprinkle with crumb mixture if you wish.

    Toasted Crumbs: Heat the 2 tablespoons oil in a small skillet and stir with bread crumbs until toasty. Sprinkle over salmon mixture.

SEAFOOD PUFF

SERVES 4

    3 large matzo squares or a sleeve of unsalted soda crackers

    4 servings canned tuna, sardines, or other seafood, drained

    1 can of French-fried onions

    Small can of evaporated milk (⅔ cup)

    ⅓ cup water

    2 eggs or equivalent

    ½ teaspoon each dried thyme, dry mustard powder

Grease an 8 x 8-inch baking pan and line the bottom with matzo or soda crackers. Add a layer of seafood, another layer of cracker, remaining seafood and a final layer of cracker. Sprinkle with onion rings to taste. (You may not use the entire can.) Whisk milk, water, eggs, thyme, and mustard and pour over the dish. Let it stand 20 minutes. Bake 30 to 40 minutes at 350°F until filling sets, as for custard.

More Uses for Canned Seafood

Don't forget such comfort food classics as tuna-noodle hot dish, tuna salad, tuna melts, and creamed tuna to serve over what have you. Canned salmon stalwarts include salmon loaf or salmon patties. Canned clam chowder, fortified with extra tuna or salmon, also makes a suitable main dish.

Rolled dough with filling can create dishes for almost any course of the meal. Bundles can be baked, fried, deep fried, or cooked over a campfire in pie irons.

Meatless Main Dishes

BROWNED PINEAPPLE BULGUR BURGOO
SERVES 4–6

> 20-ounce can pineapple tidbits, drained
>
> 3 tablespoons dried onion bits
>
> 2 tablespoons canola oil
>
> 1 tablespoon curry powder
>
> 1 teaspoon garlic salt
>
> 2 teaspoons dried cilantro
>
> 2 cups water
>
> ½ cup liquid
>
> 2 vegetable bouillon cubes
>
> 1 or 2 cans, 19 ounces each, large white beans
>
> 1 cup bulgur

Drain pineapple into a ½-cup measure and add onion bits to soak. Add water to make ½ cup liquid. Set aside. Heat the oil in a saucepan or large skillet and sauté the drained pineapple until lightly browned, gradually stirring in curry powder, garlic salt, and cilantro to coat well. Add the 2 cups water, bouillon, and the liquid with onions and bring to a boil. Stir in beans with their liquid and bring back to a boil. Remove from heat and stir in bulgur. Cover and set aside 20 minutes while bulgur softens. Stir and serve.

TOMATO-CORN CASSEROLE

SERVES 4–6

Instead of bread crumbs you might use croutons or diced, stale bread with added Italian seasoning.

> 2 cans, 10 ounces each, whole kernel corn with peppers (Mexi-corn), undrained
>
> 2 cans, 15 ounces each, diced tomatoes with onion and pepper, undrained
>
> 1 tablespoon balsamic vinegar
>
> 2 cups Italian seasoned bread crumbs
>
> ¼ cup olive oil
>
> 1 cup grated Parmesan cheese

Spray or oil a 9 x 13-inch casserole. Mix vegetables in the casserole. Add balsamic vinegar. Top with bread crumbs. Drizzle with olive oil. Sprinkle with cheese. Bake at 350°F or in a solar cooker until heated through.

MUSHROOM CREAM

SERVES 4

Don't skimp on the mushrooms. They're the meat substitute here, so you need a total of at least two cups.

> 16- to 20-ounce can of mushrooms, drained, OR 2 cups reconstituted, cooked dried mushrooms
>
> 2 tablespoons olive oil
>
> 1 tablespoon Worcestershire sauce
>
> 2 teaspoons tarragon vinegar OR
> > 2 teaspoons cider vinegar and ½ teaspoon dried tarragon
>
> 7.6-ounce tin of cream

In a large skillet, sizzle mushrooms in hot oil until they begin to brown. Stir in remaining ingredients in the order listed. Heat through, but do not boil. Serve over the starch of your choice.

EMERALD RICE

SERVES 3–6

For some cooks this will be a side dish, but a generous amount of cheese can also make it a vegetarian main dish. Midori is a green, melon-flavored liqueur that imparts a beguiling sweetness to the dish.

> 2 tablespoons Midori liqueur OR 2 tablespoons strong, brewed green tea
>
> 3 tablespoons dried onion bits
>
> 4 tablespoons dried sweet bell pepper flakes
>
> 2 tablespoons freeze-dried chives
>
> 4 tablespoons dried parsley flakes
>
> ¼ cup extra virgin olive oil
>
> 2 cups raw rice
>
> 4 cups water
>
> 3 vegetable bouillon cubes
>
> ¼ cup freeze-dried English peas
>
> 1 to 1½ cups grated dry cheese, such as Parmesan

In a small container, soak onion in the tea or Midori. In a saucepan or pressure cooker, stir rice into hot oil until well coated. Add water, onion, bouillon, and vegetables. Serves 3 as a main dish, 6 as a side dish.

Pressure cooker method: Bring to full pressure for one minute (3 minutes for brown rice). Turn off heat and let pressure return to normal. Stir in cheese and serve.

Saucepan method: Proceed as above, bring to a boil, cover, and reduce heat. Cook over low heat (do not peek or stir) for 20 minutes for white rice, 30 minutes for brown rice. Fold in cheese and serve.

TORTELLINI À LA DRY TORTUGAS

SERVES 4–5

Fort Jefferson in the Dry Tortugas is one of the world's best places to camp or anchor, but there are no supplies there. Take everything you need including water. Serve this hearty main dish warm, at room temperature, or chilled. It's possible to make tortellini from scratch using only shelf-stable ingredients, but packages are so much easier.

> 8-ounce package dry three-cheese tortellini
>
> Small can sliced ripe olives, well drained
>
> Small can marinated artichoke hearts, chopped
>
> Small can diced water chestnuts, drained
>
> Small can caponata (eggplant appetizer)
>
> 1 tablespoon red wine vinegar
>
> ¼ cup vegetable oil
>
> 1 jar Old English cheese spread
>
> Dried parsley flakes

Cook and drain tortellini according to package directions. Toss it with olives, undrained artichoke hearts, caponata, and water chestnuts. Mix vinegar and oil and fold into tortellini mixture. Arrange on plates and use two spoons to garnish with small flecks of the cheese spread. Sprinkle with parsley flakes.

CORN CASSEROLE

SERVES 4–6

> Small can evaporated milk (⅔ cup)
>
> ¼ cup water
>
> 2 tablespoons prepared mustard
>
> 1 tablespoon soy sauce
>
> ¼ cup diced, dried onions
>
> 4 eggs or equivalent
>
> 15-ounce can of cream-style corn
>
> 15-ounce can of whole kernel corn, undrained
>
> 1½ cups packaged dry bread crumbs
>
> ¼ cup olive oil

Combine milk, water, mustard, and soy sauce. Add dried onions and set aside to soak. Oil or spray a 9 x 12-inch baking dish. Add corn. Mix eggs and bread crumbs into the milk mixture and spoon over the corn. Drizzle with olive oil. Bake 35 to 45 minutes or until the crumb topping is firm and golden.

Optional: Drain a can of lima beans and mix with the corn.

PLENTIFUL POLENTA

SERVES 4–6

Hot, creamy, freshly made polenta can be spread on a plate and used as an underpinning for a sauce. When sliced and fried it develops a different flavor and texture.

> 2 cups prepared polenta
>
> About ½ cup flour
>
> 1 teaspoon each salt, pepper, Italian seasoning
>
> 3 tablespoons vegetable oil
>
> 1 can or jar of your favorite spaghetti sauce (about 3 cups)
>
> 6-ounce can caponata (eggplant appetizer)
>
> Small can sliced ripe olives, well drained
>
> Grated Parmesan

Follow package directions to make polenta. Spread it in a greased pan and let it cool until solid. Chill if possible. Cut it in slices or squares. Dip polenta slices in flour seasoned with salt, pepper, and Italian seasoning and cook in hot oil until it's crusty on both sides. Place on plates. Working quickly over high heat, put spaghetti sauce, olives, and eggplant appetizer in the same skillet and heat, stirring, until it's bubbly. Spoon over polenta and pass the grated cheese.

Cook's note: Polenta may be too soft to slice, especially if you have no refrigeration. Form it into patties, dip in flour, and proceed.

HAITIAN BEAN GRAVY

Make this authentic folk dish with almost any dried beans you have on hand (black, navy, great northern, pinto, etc.) In wealthier Haitian homes the "gravy" is puréed in a blender and served over rice. In poorer homes it's mashed as fine as possible and served over cornmeal mush, also known as cornmeal porridge.

> 1½ cups dried beans
>
> Water to cover
>
> 1 tablespoon vegetable oil, butter, bacon drippings, or lard
>
> 1 tablespoon each dried garlic granules, dried onion bits
>
> ½ teaspoon ground cloves
>
> Small onion, diced
>
> A few grinds of fresh pepper
>
> 1 tablespoon additional fat or oil

Wash and pick over beans. Cover with water and soak overnight. Drain and cover with water. Bring to a boil and add fat and seasonings. Bring back to a boil and cover. Reduce heat and simmer until beans are very, very tender. You may have to add water to keep them from burning, but do cook them to a mush.

Drain and mash beans, returning enough liquid to the mixture to make a thick gravy. Stir in additional fat or cayenne and fat or oil and spoon over rice or whatever starch you have.

Chapter 6

Sustaining Soups

On the Beaufort Scale of comfort foods, soups are a Force 12. In plentiful times soup is a first course or a satisfying lunch. In lean times soups can be thinned with water, bouillon, milk, tomato juice, or broth to assure a serving for everyone.

SWEET POTATO SOUP FOR ONE

Ounce for ounce, baby food is a budget bummer, but the small portions make it a good choice for some singles some of the time. Serve this sip-able soup in an oversize mug. No spoon required.

> ⅔ cup water
>
> 1 bouillon cube (vegetable, chicken, or beef)
>
> 1 jar puréed carrot baby food (4 ounces)
>
> 1 jar puréed sweet potato baby food (4 ounces)
>
> Curry powder to taste

Bring water to a boil and stir in bouillon to dissolve. Stir in baby foods with curry to taste. Heat through. Makes about 1½ cups soup.

Put a pat of butter and a sprinkling of herbs in each bowl before adding soup.
They float to the top, putting a pretty patina on the presentation.

SEAFOOD POTAGE FOR SINGLES

How big is one serving? For the active sailor, backpacker, explorer, and hunter it's far larger than a meal for a desk jockey. This thick, hearty stew is just right for a loner who is snowed in or for the single-hander who is sailing the Roaring Forties.

> ¾ cup water
>
> 1 packet of butter flavor instant grits
>
> ½ teaspoon garlic powder
>
> 1 teaspoon onion powder
>
> Boiling water
>
> 16- to 18-ounce can of ready-to-eat New England–style clam chowder
>
> Dried parsley or chives

Bring water to a boil and stir in grits, garlic, and onion. Stir in clam chowder and heat, stirring, over medium/low flame until heated through. Sprinkle with dried parsley flakes or chives. Makes one large or two medium servings.

BULLY BEEF SOUP

SERVES 6–10

For generations, canned corned beef has been a pantry stalwart. It's salty, so additional ingredients should be no- and low-salt.

> 12-ounce can of corned beef
>
> ⅓ cup dried onion bits
>
> 5 cups water
>
> 28- to 32-ounce can of diced tomatoes, undrained
>
> ½ cup pearl barley or brown rice
>
> ½ cup rinsed lentils
>
> 1 teaspoon dried Italian seasoning (or more to taste)
>
> 1 teaspoon fresh ground pepper
>
> 1 or 2 cans, 15 ounces each, mixed vegetables, undrained

Scrape and discard visible fat from the corned beef. Put corned beef in a 6-quart kettle with the water and dried onions. Let stand a few minutes for onions to soak. Break up beef with a fork. It will break up further during cooking. Add tomatoes, lentils, and barley or rice. Bring to a boil, stir, cover, reduce heat, and simmer at least 30 minutes or until lentils and rice/barley are tender. Stir in mixed vegetables to heat through. Add water or broth if a thinner soup is desired.

Bouillon comes in cubes, pastes, and powders to save space. Broth is available full strength or concentrated in tins and aseptic packaging.

DOLCE VITA WEDDING SOUP

SERVES 4

This is another pantry-ized version of a classic European recipe. Traditionally, Italian Wedding Soup is made with spinach, so use that instead of the green beans if you have it.

12-ounce can of sliced roast beef in gravy

¼ cup dried onion bits

1 teaspoon dried garlic granules

15-ounce can of sliced carrots, undrained

15-ounce can of sliced green beans, undrained

1 quart low-sodium chicken or beef broth

½ cup orzo pasta

1 tablespoon mixed Italian seasoning, divided

1 large egg or equivalent reconstituted powdered egg

⅓ cup dry bread crumbs

3 tablespoons grated Parmesan cheese

Drain the roast beef into a measure and add water if needed to make ½ cup. Stir in onion and garlic bits and set aside to soak. Put beef in a bowl and break it up into shreds. Stir in a teaspoon of Italian seasoning, bread crumbs, cheese, and egg. Set aside.

In a saucepan bring carrots, green beans, broth, drained onion, garlic, and 2 teaspoons Italian seasoning to a boil. Stir in orzo. Reduce heat, but keep at an active simmer for 5 minutes. Using two teaspoons, shape little meatballs with the beef mixture and drop gently into the soup. Cover and cook without stirring over low heat 8 to 10 minutes until orzo is tender and meatballs are firm.

GET WELL SOUP 1

MAKES 4½ cups

One of the most gentle soups, this recipe is a snap to stir up any time, especially when someone is on the sick list. It's based on classic Italian Stracciatella, or Egg Drop Soup. Here's how.

> One-quart carton chicken broth OR 4 chicken flavor bouillon cubes plus 4 cups water
>
> 1 tablespoon water
>
> 2 eggs or equivalent
>
> 1 tablespoon cornstarch
>
> Salt, pepper, dried parsley flakes

Set aside about ⅓ cup of the chicken stock or water and heat the rest to boiling. Whisk eggs with the tablespoon of water. Using a long-handled spoon, swirl the boiling stock while slowly stirring in eggs in a thin stream. Stir cornstarch into the cold, ⅓ cup water or stock until smooth, then stir into boiling soup. Season to taste, but keep it bland if it's for the sickroom.

GET WELL SOUP II

SERVES 5

You've heard jokes about the soup called gruel. It really was a sickroom staple in olden times, and it can come in handy today in survival situations. It's simply a starch plus liquid and perhaps a very mild flavoring such as sugar. This recipe is adapted from an old cookbook that had four gruel recipes (farina, oatmeal, arrowroot, and cornmeal, which was then called Indian meal). Don't overdo it with the butter, salt, and sugar. Keep it bland until the patient feels better.

> 2 cups cold water
>
> ½ cup rolled oats
>
> 1 scant teaspoon butter or olive oil
>
> 1 teaspoon (or more to taste) sugar
>
> Pinch salt
>
> ½ cup milk

Stir oatmeal into boiling water and cook until oatmeal is very soft. Stir in butter or oil, sugar, salt, and milk. Mixture will be thin. This can be sipped from a mug if the patient is able, or feed it by the lovin' spoonful. Makes 5 servings of ½ cup each.

BORSHT WITH DILL DUMPLINGS

SERVES 6–8

Beets add bulk and sweetness to canned beef in this takeoff on a classic European soup. For a meatier soup you can add a 12-ounce can of corned beef.

> 2 cans, 15 ounces each, beets (preferably julienne style), undrained
>
> 16-ounce jar of sweet and sour red cabbage
>
> 15-ounce can ready-to-serve beef broth
>
> 15-ounce can of diced tomatoes with juice
>
> ¼ teaspoon ground cloves
>
> 1 teaspoon ground cinnamon
>
> 12-ounce can roast beef with gravy
>
> 1½ cups biscuit mix
>
> ½ teaspoon dill weed
>
> Water or milk

If you can't find julienne beets, buy whole canned beets. It's quick and easy to grate them or chop fine. In a large saucepan combine beets, beet juice, broth, tomatoes, seasoning, and broken up roast beef and gravy. In a bowl, stir biscuit mix and dill weed with enough water or milk to make a thick dough. Drop by teaspoons on actively simmering soup and cook 10 minutes uncovered, 10 minutes tightly covered. Serve at once.

SAUCY TOMATO SOUP

SERVES 6–8

This hearty soup cooks over any fire or campstove in a jiffy.

> 12-ounce package orzo or other small pasta
>
> 2 jars or cans, 26 ounces each, tomato-basil spaghetti sauce
>
> 4 cups water
>
> 4 bouillon cubes (vegetable, chicken, or beef)
>
> Handful of freeze-dried kale
>
> Parmesan cheese (optional)

Cook the pasta until just al dente. Pour off much of the water, but leave it soupy. Then stir in the spaghetti sauce, water, and bouillon. Bring to a boil, stir in the kale, and cook just until the kale is tender. Ladle into soup bowls and top each serving with Parmesan cheese.

CANNERY ROW FISH CHOWDER

SERVES 6

> 1 box scalloped potato mix
> 4 cups water
> 15-ounce can salmon
> 15-ounce can cream-style corn
> 1 teaspoon dried, crumbled thyme
> ½ teaspoon celery seed (not celery salt)
> 12-ounce can of evaporated milk

Bring juice from the salmon plus four cups water to a boil. Add dried potatoes and the flavoring packet. Cover, reduce heat, and simmer until potatoes are tender. (About 40 minutes on the stove or 2 minutes under full pressure.)

Discard salmon skin, break up fish, and mash bones. Add to the pot with the corn, celery seed, and thyme. Bring to a boil, turn off heat, and stir in evaporated milk. Serve at once.

DEEP SEA SOUP WITH DUMPLINGS

SERVES 6

Use condensed, homemade, or ready-to-serve soup as long as it adds up to about 6 cups of clam chowder. Manhattan-style clam chowder is tomato-based. Do not use New England clam chowder, which is milk-based.

> 6 cups Manhattan-style clam chowder
>
> 2 cups tomato or Clamato juice, water, broth, or bouillon
>
> 1½ cups biscuit mix
>
> ½ teaspoon sweet paprika
>
> 1 teaspoon dried parsley flakes
>
> Milk or water
>
> Small can shrimp, drained (optional)

While chowder and extra juice or bouillon come to a steady simmer (not a hard boil) in a large saucepan, mix parsley flakes and paprika with biscuit mix. Add milk or water to make a thick dough. Do not overbeat. Cut up shrimp and fold into dough.

Drop dough by teaspoons into simmering chowder and cook 10 minutes uncovered, then 10 minutes tightly covered. Serve at once.

One pot and a clever combination of cans make a substantial one-pot soup meal.

The Ultimate Soup Mix

Buy ingredients for this hearty soup and then make up enough mixes to last through the entire cruise, camping trip, or season at your fish camp. These measurements make soup for four. Double up for a larger family or pare down for a smaller family. Unlike bean soup mixes, this one requires no soaking and it cooks in 30 to 45 minutes at most (or 10 minutes in the pressure cooker).

The mixture can be varied with more of this, less of that. *Just do not add any dried beans that require soaking.*

Shopping list:

1 bag dried yellow split peas

1 bag small dried lima beans

1 bag dried green split peas

1 bag brown lentils

1 bag red or yellow lentils

1 bag brown rice, oat groats, ferro, or barley

Mix well and keep in a cool, dry place. Store it one container or package it in batches. Each cup of the mix makes soup for four people.

(continued)

TURTLE SOUP

SERVES 6–8

Tortellini means "little turtles," and they swim deliciously in this vegetarian soup. It's warming and filling—a quick meal from your prepared pantry.

6 to 8 cups water

5 to 7 vegetable bouillon cubes

1 teaspoon dried Italian seasoning

20-ounce package shelf-stable three-cheese tortellini

14-ounce can artichoke hearts, drained and cut up

The Ultimate Soup Mix (continued)

To make soup:

Measure a cup of the mixture, remove any foreign matter, and rinse well. Bring 4 cups water to a boil and stir in mix plus one or more of the following ingredients:

2 to 4 bouillon cubes or teaspoons of powdered bouillon

1 tablespoon dried parsley

1 to 2 tablespoons dried onion bits

2 tablespoons small pasta or fine noodles

1 teaspoon dried garlic granules

1 teaspoon celery seed, crumbled dry basil, or crumbled dried oregano

Canned diced tomatoes

1 to 2 tablespoons snipped sun-dried tomatoes

Cover, lower heat, and simmer 30 to 45 minutes or until everything is tender. Stir well and adjust seasonings. Ladle into soup bowls.

15-ounce can carrots, drained and coarsely chopped OR
1½ cups reconstituted dried diced carrots

12-ounce package firm tofu, finely diced (optional)

Bring water to a boil with five bouillon cubes and Italian seasoning. Add tortellini and cook 6 minutes. Keep the pot boiling while gradually adding artichoke hearts and carrots. The tortellini should be tender after 8 minutes. Stir in the tofu to heat through. Taste and add more bouillon if it's needed, plus another cup or two of water if you want a thinner soup. Ladle into soup bowls.

SPLIT PEA SOUP

SERVES 6–8

This is a perfect soup to cook long and slow over a campfire. It's as satisfying as bean soup, but peas don't require soaking and they cook in a fraction of the time. This soup may also be made in a solar cooker or a slow cooker, on a camp stove, or in a pressure cooker. The standard rule of filling a pressure cooker no more than ⅔ full is especially important when making bean and pea soup.

> 16-ounce bag split peas, rinsed and picked over
>
> 8 cups water
>
> 10-ounce can chunk ham, broken up
>
> ¼ cup dried onion bits
>
> 1 teaspoon dried thyme
>
> 1 bay leaf
>
> 1 teaspoon dried garlic granules
>
> 15-ounce can carrots, drained and cut up
>
> Salt and pepper to taste
>
> *Optional:* Up to 1 cup white wine, broth, or water
>
> *Garnish:* Tinned cream (optional)
> Hot sauce (optional)

Put water, peas, and ham in a soup pot. Add onions, thyme, bay leaf, and garlic. Bring to a boil, cover, reduce heat, and simmer until peas are very tender. Stir in carrots to heat through. Season to taste, remove bay leaf, and serve. Pass the hot sauce. On standing, soup will thicken. Thin it with white wine, broth, milk, or water.

To put a flourish on the presentation, ladle soup into bowls and spoon a dollop of heavy cream in the middle. Use a spoon handle or narrow knife to run through the cream in a spiral or zigzag pattern.

PASTA-MATO SOUP

SERVES 6–8

By using vegetable pasta or spinach macaroni you add color as well as veggie nutrition.

6 cups water

2 cups vegetable pasta

2 bouillon cubes (chicken, vegetable, or beef) OR
    2 teaspoons powdered or paste bouillon

2 cans or jars, 26 to 32 ounces each, spaghetti sauce

Dried parsley

Grated Parmesan cheese

Bring water to a boil and cook pasta until it's al dente. Do not drain. Stir in bouillon cubes until they dissolve, then stir in spaghetti sauce. Ladle into soup bowls, sprinkle with dried parsley, and shower with grated cheese.

Cook's note: For a heartier soup, add a can of kidney beans. For more color, add a can of mixed vegetables.

Chapter 7

Salads from Your Shelf

One of the biggest challenges for the pantry chef is to make salads that have eye appeal, texture contrast, and fresh taste. Water chestnuts are one of the few foods that survive the canning process without losing their crunch. You can also make sprouts for a fresh taste or add croutons for crispness. Salads add variety to a meal and are also a way to get extra vitamins and fiber.

Main-Dish Salads

TUSCANY TUNA SALAD

SERVES 4–8

This stout salad has tang, taste and attitude yet all ingredients come from the shelf.

> 2 cans, 5 to 6 ounces each, solid pack tuna in water
>
> 1 teaspoon dried garlic granules
>
> 1 tablespoon dried onion bits
>
> Small can sliced black olives, drained
>
> 2-ounce jar diced pimentos, drained
>
> 1 tablespoon capers, drained
>
> About ⅔ cup chopped, stuffed olives, drained
>
> 2 tablespoons chopped anchovy
>
> 1 teaspoon dried oregano
>
> ⅓ cup extra-virgin olive oil (or more to taste)
>
> Freshly ground black pepper

Drain canned tuna into a small container. Add dried garlic and onion bits and let them soak while you assemble the salad. In a bowl, break up tuna and stir in black olives, pimentos, capers, anchovy, and oregano. Fold in olive oil, softened onion and garlic bits, and freshly ground pepper to taste. Serve as is or use as a sandwich filling. Makes 4 main dish portions or 6 to 8 sandwiches.

ORZO SALAD

SERVES 4

> 3 cups water
>
> 2 teaspoons chicken soup base or powdered chicken bouillon
>
> 1 cup orzo
>
> 2 tablespoons sun-dried tomatoes in oil, chopped
>
> Small can sliced black olives, well drained
>
> ½ cup stuffed green olives, chopped
>
> ½ cup (or to taste) diced pepperoni, jerky, or other shelf-stable sausage
>
> Bottled or homemade red wine vinaigrette to taste
>
> ½ cup grated Parmesan cheese or other grated hard cheese

Bring water and bouillon to a boil. Add orzo and cook until tender. Turn off heat and let stand, covered, until it won't absorb any more broth. Drain any excess broth. Mix cooled orzo with tomatoes, olives, meat, and vinaigrette to taste. Sprinkle with cheese.

Vegan version: Substitute vegetable bouillon, eliminate meat and cheese, and add a drained, rinsed can of chickpeas.

RICE AND BEAN SALAD YOUR WAY

SERVES 4

Make this main dish salad meaty, vegetarian, or vegan. Use your choice of rice (brown, red, basmati, jasmine) and add-ons, then serve it warm, at room temperature, or chilled.

> 4 cups cooked rice
>
> 14.5-ounce can diced tomatoes, drained
>
> 15-ounce can black beans or kidney beans, rinsed and drained
>
> Your favorite vinaigrette

Suggested Additions

> Chopped nuts
>
> Diced, drained water chestnuts
>
> Diced tofu
>
> Grated cheese
>
> Drained mushroom slices
>
> Chopped, stuffed olives
>
> Small can chilies, drained
>
> Snipped pepperoni or jerky
>
> Real or imitation bacon bits

Fold rice, tomatoes, and black beans together with add-ons of choice and toss lightly with vinaigrette to taste.

OPEN SESAME NOODLE SALAD

SERVES 6–8

To make this a vegetarian dish, omit the chicken and substitute 2 cups diced, extra-firm tofu.

> 16-ounce package thin spaghetti
>
> ⅓ cup rice vinegar

Pasta salads from the shelf add color and tang to a simple meal.

¼ cup low-sodium soy sauce

¼ cup olive oil

1 teaspoon ground ginger

2 tablespoons dark sesame oil

Small can diced water chestnuts, well drained

15-ounce can baby corn, well drained

2 cans, 10 ounces each, chunk chicken OR
    2 cups reconstituted diced chicken

Black or golden sesame seeds

While spaghetti cooks according to package directions, whisk vinegar, soy sauce, olive oil, ginger, and sesame oil. Drain spaghetti and fold in dressing mixture, water chestnuts, baby corn, and chicken. Serve now or let it cool. Sprinkle with sesame seeds.

Side-Dish Salads

CRAZY QUILT SALAD

SERVES 6–8

> 2 cups macaroni or other small pasta
>
> 2 tablespoons dried onion bits
>
> 1 tablespoon dried green pepper bits
>
> ⅓ cup olive oil
>
> 2 tablespoons red wine vinegar
>
> Small jar sliced, stuffed olives, well drained
>
> 8-ounce can of whole kernel corn*
>
> 8-ounce can of diced or stewed tomatoes
>
> 1 tablespoon red wine vinegar or more to taste
>
> Freshly ground pepper

Cook pasta in boiling water with the onion and green pepper. Drain pasta and stir in olive oil and vinegar while it's hot. Fold in olives, corn, and tomatoes. Let stand 5 to 10 minutes, stir, and add pepper to taste, with more vinegar if desired. Serve warm, at room temperature, or chilled. Turn it into a main dish by adding diced cheese, tofu, or cooked meat.

   * *Juice from the corn can be part of the water measure used for cooking pasta.*

Color and Crunch

When you need a bit of color and texture to complete a meal, these pantry staples can be called in.

- Stewed, diced tomatoes sprinkled with dried chives
- Dilly beans
- Pickled beets
- Salsa, chili sauce
- Toothpick kebabs with pickled onions, stuffed olives, pickles
- Sauerkraut
- Sweet 'n sour red cabbage from a jar
- Cranberry sauce
- Chunky applesauce
- Giardiniera (Italian pickled vegetables also called sottaceti)

Check supermarket shelves and ethnic grocery stores for specialty condiments such as chow-chow, relishes, chutneys, kimchi, salted radish, gefilte fish, mojos, and so on.

Splurge occasionally on specialty condiments to hang a ruffle on a bland pantry meal.

FANDANGO SALAD

SERVES 6

> 15-ounce can of whole kernel corn, drained
>
> 15-ounce jar of your favorite salsa
>
> 15-ounce jar of black bean and corn salsa
>
> Dry lemon or lime flavor gelatin dessert mix
>
> Seasonings to taste

Mix corn and salsas. Add dry gelatin dessert mix one teaspoon at a time to taste. Add salt and pepper to taste.

Cook's note: What to do with leftover gelatin dessert mix? Use it sparingly as a flavoring ingredient or add a cup of boiling water per scant teaspoon to make a hot drink.

ASIAN RICE SALAD

SERVES 3–4

Canned Chinese vegetables as sold in North American supermarkets are a poor substitute for fresh, but they are a colorful and varied mix for the occasional change of pace when you're living on stowed food supplies. Rice is available in many flavors and forms including ready-to-eat rice in shelf-stable pouches.

> 1 cup unseasoned cooked rice
>
> ⅔ cup bottled Asian-style salad dressing (more or less to taste)
>
> 15-ounce can mixed Chinese vegetables, drained
>
> Small can sliced mushrooms, drained
>
> Small can sliced or diced water chestnuts, drained
>
> ½ cup sliced almonds

Put the salad dressing in a bowl and stir in rice. Fold in vegetables. Arrange on plates and sprinkle with sliced almonds.

Cook's note: To make a larger salad, add a can of drained baby corn and more dressing to taste. To turn this into a main dish salad, add a can of chunk chicken.

CARROT-PINEAPPLE SALAD

SERVES 5–6

This recipe has tang, sweetness, and texture contrast—most welcome when you're living on shelf-stable ingredients.

> 2 cans, 15 ounces each, julienne carrots, drained, OR
>> 2 cans carrots, drained and chopped
>
> 1 teaspoon lemon flavor gelatin dessert mix (or more to taste)
>
> Small can crushed pineapple
>
> 1 cup shredded coconut
>
> ½ cup raisins
>
> ¼ cup French dressing or other sweet salad dressing

Toss carrots with lemon gelatin. Drain pineapple. Fold everything together with enough dressing to moisten.

Cook's note: For an adult meal, heat ¼ cup rum to steaming and pour over raisins. Let soak until cool, then add to the salad.

Chapter 8

Backup Breads and Substitute Spreads

Bread Is Basic

Bread for toast. Bread for sandwiches. Bread crumbs. Diced bread for croutons. It's hard to imagine life without "our daily bread," but there is no more difficult item to come by during emergencies. Bread is one of the first items to be swept off supermarket shelves when a snowstorm is forecast. It doesn't keep well, so your current supplies are soon gone, yet it takes time and resources to bake yeast breads. Provisioning this staple is a tall order.

Most of these recipes can be made as a loaf or in individual portions, such as in muffin tins. Yeast dough can be shaped around a toasting fork to cook over a campfire or flattened in the palm to cook on a griddle (think pita bread). One of the easiest ways to make dough is to stir a 12-ounce can of beer into 3 cups of self-rising flour and bake it in the oven, a skillet, a campfire, or a covered grill. It has the taste of yeast without the hassle.

These breads can round out pantry menus.

BASIC YEAST BREAD

Yeast is a living organism, fussy about environment. It takes energy to knead the dough, moist heat to raise it, dry heat to bake it. Practice makes perfect when it comes to learning the feel of dough, how to gauge when it's "double in bulk," and how to know when the loaf is done. If homemade bread is part of your provisioning plan, here's how to get started:

> 1 cup warm water (not too hot)
>
> 1 tablespoon active dry yeast
>
> 1 tablespoon honey or sugar
>
> About 3 cups flour (white or whole wheat or some of each)
>
> 1 teaspoon salt
>
> 1 tablespoon vegetable oil

Set the oven to 375°F. In a bowl stir water with yeast and honey. Let stand 5 minutes. Stir in some of the flour with the salt and oil. Continue to stir in flour until dough is firm, then turn out on a floured linen towel and knead in more flour until dough is no longer sticky. Put dough in a greased bowl, cover, and let rise in a warm place until it's double in bulk. Knead, shape into a loaf or loaves, and let rise until doubled. Bake 35 minutes or until temperature reaches 190°F.

BASIC SODA BREAD

Have hot, crusty bread on the table tonight without tiresome rising. Mix it, knead it just a little, and bake it in one large or two small loaves. Some recipes for Irish Soda Bread call for a tablespoon of caraway seed or a half cup of raisins.

> 4 cups flour
>
> 1 tablespoon baking powder
>
> 1 teaspoon baking soda
>
> 1 teaspoon salt
>
> 2 cups reconstituted milk AND 2 teaspoons vinegar OR
> 2 cups buttermilk

Stir vinegar into milk and let it stand a few minutes. Mix dry ingredients in a bowl. Whisk in the milk and blend only until everything is evenly moistened. Turn out on a floured surface and knead 12 to 15 times. Do not overwork dough. Form dough into one large or two small rounds on a greased or lined baking sheet. Bake 45 to 60 minutes at 350°F. Loaf will be golden brown and will sound hollow when tapped. If you insert a toothpick it should come out clean. This bread is best served warm and fresh from the oven.

Although soda bread isn't the best choice for toast or sandwiches, it will slice better if cooled, wrapped, and left to "season" overnight.

Bread is a basic staff of life yet one of the most difficult items to keep on hand.

CASSEROLE CHEESE BREAD

There's no need to knead this hearty bread. Carve slabs of warm cheese bread, open a can of soup, and supper is served. Cheese is salty. If you're on a low-sodium diet omit the extra salt.

> Small can of evaporated milk (⅔ cup)
>
> Hot water
>
> 1 tablespoon each sugar, vegetable oil, dry yeast
>
> 1 teaspoon salt (optional)
>
> 4½ cups all-purpose flour
>
> 1 cup grated sharp cheddar cheese

Stir enough hot water into the evaporated milk to make one cup. In large bowl mix the warm milk mixture, sugar, oil, and yeast. Little by little stir in flour, adding salt along the way. Fold in grated cheese. Cover bowl and let dough rise in a warm spot. Stir down and put dough in a well-greased 1½-quart baking pan or loaf pan(s). Let it rise to double in size and bake at 350°F about one hour or until golden and crusty.

Turn out of the pan and chop in chunks to serve warm. For sliced bread, cool loaves and wrap overnight.

CRUMPETS

Like English muffins, crumpets satisfy a craving for yeast bread. However, they are a batter rather than a dough, cooked like pancakes within a ring mold. Traditional crumpet rings are cast iron and have a handle, but you could use round biscuit or cookie cutters or tuna cans with tops and bottoms removed.

> 2½ cups warm water
>
> ½ cup dry milk powder
>
> 1 tablespoon sugar
>
> 2 teaspoons active dry yeast
>
> 2⅔ cups flour
>
> 1 teaspoon each salt, baking soda

Stir yeast, milk, and sugar into half of the warm water and let stand. Mix flour, salt, and baking powder in a bowl. Stir in the yeast mixture, then add the rest of the warm water to make a batter the consistency of thick cream. Cover and let stand for an hour.

Heat a griddle or large, heavy skillet over low-medium heat. Grease the insides of the crumpet rings well and set them on the griddle or skillet. Pour batter into rings until they are half full. Bake about 4 minutes or until browned on one side. Slip crumpets out of rings, flip, and brown the other side. They can be eaten as is or split and toasted.

English muffin variation: Use half the amount of water or twice the flour to make a dough thick enough to handle. After it rises, pat it out on a linen towel heavily dusted with cornmeal. Cut individual rounds, sprinkle tops with cornmeal, and bake on a griddle to brown both sides. Split and toast.

Both English muffins and crumpets are yeast breads baked on a griddle.

CONFETTI CREPES

MAKES 20 CREPES

Crepes go faster if you keep two or more 8-inch skillets going at once. Rice gives these crepes more structure.

> 1 cup rice, preferably a mixture of different types and colors
>
> 2 cups water
>
> 8 eggs or equivalent
>
> 1 cup flour
>
> 2 tablespoons vegetable oil
>
> 2 teaspoons each salt, sugar

Cook rice in water 30 minutes and drain any excess water. Rice should be tender and very dry. Stir with a fork to fluff it and let it cool. Beat eggs and stir in flour, oil, salt, sugar, and rice. Lightly grease skillets and add ⅓ cup batter. Quickly tilt pan to cover it with a thin coating of batter. When crepes brown on one side, brown the other side.

Spread crepes with sweet or savory stuffing such as fruit pie filling, chili, creamed chicken, or cheese sauce. Serve hot.

CHICKPEA CRACKERS

> 2 cups chickpea flour, also called garbanzo flour
>
> ½ teaspoon salt
>
> ¼ cup water (or more if needed)
>
> Vegetable oil
>
> *Optional:*
>
> 1 teaspoon each ground cumin, black pepper, garlic powder

Mix dry ingredients and add water to make a firm, dry dough. Add a little more water if necessary. Knead the dough about five minutes or until smooth. Pinch off 12 pieces and roll each as thin as possible. Brush lightly with oil and bake on a griddle until crisp and dry or in the oven at 300°F for 20 to 25 minutes. When warm and pliable they make good wraps. When cooled they're good with dips or spreads.

MUSHROOM SCONES

SERVES 6

Mushrooms add extra pow to baking powder biscuits. Add a mug of soup and you have a substantial meal.

> Small can mushroom bits and pieces, well drained OR 1 cup reconstituted and cooked dried mushrooms
>
> 2 tablespoons diced dried onion bits
>
> 2 tablespoons water, broth, or wine
>
> ½ cup butter or shortening
>
> 2 cups self-rising flour
>
> 2 tablespoons grated dry cheese such as Parmesan (optional)
>
> Milk or water

Drain mushrooms. Soak onion bits in water, broth, or wine for 10 minutes or more. Cut butter or shortening into self-rising flour and cheese. Add enough milk to make a thick dough. Stir in mushrooms and drained onion bits. Turn out dough on a floured paper towel, knead half a dozen times, and form into a circle ½ inch thick.

Score circle into 6 wedges and bake on a greased cookie sheet at 400°F for 12 to 15 minutes until golden. See Appendix for baking without an oven.

MEXI-DIXIE SPOON BREAD

Add sombrero sizzle to traditional Southern spoon bread. This moist, eggy bread is substantial enough to make a vegetarian main dish, although it's usually served as a side dish. And yes, spoon bread is served with a spoon.

>   15-ounce can cream-style corn
>
>   12-ounce can evaporated milk
>
>   Water
>
>   ¼ cup vegetable oil
>
>   1 cup yellow cornmeal
>
>   3 eggs or equivalent in reconstituted powdered eggs
>
>   1 teaspoon each baking powder, salt
>
>   4.5-ounce can diced green chiles, drained

Grease an 8- or 9-inch baking pan and preheat oven to 350°F. Add water to canned milk to make 2 cups. Stir together corn, cornmeal, milk, oil, and eggs. Let stand 10 to 15 minutes and stir in baking powder, salt, and chiles. Pour batter into the pan and bake at 350°F for an hour or until it's browned on top and "set" as for custard. Let stand 5 minutes. Serve as is or with warm cheese sauce.

FESTIVALS

SERVES 4

In Jamaica, cornbread is Johnny Cake. Festivals are a similar product that is fried. Think Hush Puppies without the spices. Serve Festivals as a bread with almost any course.

>   1 cup each flour, yellow cornmeal
>
>   2 teaspoons baking powder
>
>   1 tablespoon sugar
>
>   ½ teaspoon salt
>
>   Oil for deep frying

Whisk dry ingredients in a bowl and add just enough cold water to make a stiff dough. Knead briefly. Shape dough into 8 to 10 logs and flatten them slightly with your hands. Brown in hot vegetable oil and nestle in paper towels to drain and keep warm.

Quick breads are just that, requiring neither yeast nor rising time. (Whitney Merritt)

Substitute Spreads

Powdered, canned, and freeze-dried butter and canned ghee are available from specialty suppliers, and many other spreads and dips from the shelf can enhance your biscuits, crackers, and breads. First among them is olive oil with a splash of balsamic vinegar, a classic and delicious moistener for hearty peasant breads.

Foods to add to your pantry supplies can include nut butters, jellies, jam, preserves, bottled cheese spreads, apple or prune butter, homemade or bottled tapenade, and bottled pesto. Dehydrated cream cheese powder is available online from specialty suppliers. Just add water. Canned frosting is also a good spread for graham crackers. Canned, refried beans spread well when warmed.

HONEY BOOZE BUTTER

> ½ cup butter or butter-flavor shortening
>
> ⅓ cup each honey and brown sugar
>
> 1 teaspoon rum flavoring or brandy extract

Melt the butter or shortening and stir in honey, sugar, and extract. Let stand at room temperature until it's cool. Spread on muffins, biscuits, cookies, or graham crackers.

POLISH PORK SPREAD

Although some people avoid them for health or religious reasons, lard and other animal fats, such as schmaltz, are favored as bread spreads in many nations.

> 2 cups lard
>
> 1 tablespoon onion powder
>
> 1 teaspoon each garlic powder and an herb such as marjoram or thyme
>
> 2 drops smoke flavoring (optional)
>
> Salt and freshly ground pepper to taste

Melt lard just enough to stir in additional ingredients. Adjust seasonings to taste. Pour into a small crock or bowl. Cool and spread on bread, preferably dark rye.

BLUSHING BEAN SPREAD

Hummus, a paste made with garbanzo beans, is the classic Middle Eastern bean spread, but endless variations can be made. Here's just one of them to make with almost any canned or cooked-from-scratch dried beans: navy, pinto, kidney, lima, butterbeans, Great Northern, black beans, or even baked beans in tomato sauce.

> 3 cups drained cooked or canned beans
>
> 1 tablespoon onion powder
>
> 1 teaspoon garlic powder
>
> ½ teaspoon each black pepper, celery seed, paprika
>
> Salt to taste
>
> Optional add-ons (choose one):
>
> > Finely chopped sun-dried tomato
> >
> > 1-2 tablespoons tomato paste
> >
> > 1 tablespoon molasses
> >
> > Grated cheese
> >
> > Hot sauce

Purée beans or mash them with a fork. Mix in additional ingredients. Let stand for an hour while flavors blend. Use as a dip or spread for bread, crackers, or biscuits.

MAYONNAISE CHEESE SPREAD

This creamy spread is good cold, and it's even better when broiled as a topping for biscuits or crackers. Small jars of mayonnaise come in handy when you have no refrigeration and must use it all at once.

 2 tablespoons diced dried onion bits

 2 tablespoons white wine, broth, or water

 8-ounce jar of mayonnaise (1 cup)

 ⅓ cup grated dry cheese

 1 teaspoon dried chives and/or parsley flakes

 ⅛ teaspoon cayenne pepper (optional)

Soak dried onions in the liquid for 30 to 60 minutes. Mix everything together and spread on bread, biscuits, crackers, or crepes.

DEALER'S CHOICE BEAN SPREAD

Use any color beans you like. This meaty dip goes well with any bread, crackers, or chips you have on hand, turning them into a hearty snack or a satisfying lunch.

 15-ounce can black, kidney, pinto, red, white, or garbanzo beans

 24-ounce jar (3 cups) salsa (hot, mild, medium)

 8- to 12-ounce package pepperoni, chopped fine

 1 packet Emergen-C lemon-lime drink mix (optional) OR
  ½ teaspoon dried lemon peel (optional)

 1 teaspoon each dried cilantro, ground cumin

Rinse and drain beans. Mash finely and stir in remaining ingredients. Serve as a dip or spread.

HOT DAMN! CLAM SPREAD

This spread plus a fresh loaf of hot bread makes supper for four people.

    2 tablespoons dried onion flakes

    3 tablespoons dried green pepper flakes

    ¼ cup clam juice

    2 tablespoons olive oil

    8-ounce package process cheese such as Velveeta

    ¼ cup ketchup

    1 tablespoon Worcestershire sauce

    10-ounce can minced clams, drained

    Hot sauce to taste

Put the dried vegetables to soak in the clam juice. Put olive oil in the top of a double boiler, a heavy-bottom saucepan, or micro-ware container and add diced cheese. Cook over boiling water or low heat, stirring to melt cheese. (In the microwave cook on High, turning and stirring every 30 seconds until cheese is melted.) Stir in softened vegetables, ketchup, Worcestershire, and clams. Add hot sauce to taste. Serve warm as a dip.

WALNUT HUMMUS SPREAD

MAKES ABOUT 2 CUPS

    15-ounce can garbanzo beans, drained and rinsed

    1 cup finely chopped walnuts

    ¼ cup vegetable oil or walnut oil

    1 tablespoon balsamic vinegar

    ½ teaspoon garlic powder (not garlic salt)

    ⅛ teaspoon ground cloves

    Salt and pepper to taste

Mash beans with a fork and stir in remaining ingredients.

PIMENTO CHEESE

This combination may be strange to you unless you're from the Deep South, where pimento cheese is a popular lunch-box alternative to peanut butter and jelly, Try it as a tangy, nutritious, and colorful spread for bread or crackers, or dollop over hot vegetables. If you don't have refrigeration, make only as much as you can use at once.

12-ounce jar of grated Parmesan cheese

1 cup mayonnaise (8-ounce jar)

4-ounce jar diced pimentos, drained

Worcestershire sauce

Mix cheese and mayonnaise. Fold in pimentos and add Worcestershire to taste.

ANCHOVY SPREAD

MAKES ½ CUP

Not everyone likes anchovies, but they do provide a big burst of flavor from a very small can or tube. This easy recipe can be served on bread, tortilla chips, potato chips, rye crisp-bread, melba toast, or crackers. Try it on baked potatoes too.

2 eggs, beaten, or equivalent in reconstituted eggs

1 tablespoon vinegar or lemon juice

3 tablespoons anchovy paste

Small can anchovies, drained

Olive oil

Spray a nonstick skillet and cook eggs until just barely set. Mash eggs with a fork while adding vinegar or lemon juice and anchovy paste. Mash as finely as possible, adding a little olive oil if necessary to make a spreadable paste. Spread on bread or crackers. Garnish each portion with an anchovy. Makes about ½ cup of spread.

Chapter 9

Substantial Sides and Salvation Sauces

One-dish meals are easiest to prepare and clean up, but there are times when we have a lucky day fishing or hunting, or we splurge by opening a canned ham and surrounding it with side dishes. When you need to add a course to a meal or save a so-so dish by adding a dazzling sauce, find recipes here.

Side Dishes

When it comes to side dishes, rice is the worldwide star in the culinary crown. It's the most compact, versatile food you can carry per ounce, per inch, and per dollar. If you haven't yet discovered the many sizes, flavors, and colors of rice, do it now when you're stocking the prepared pantry.

Most rice doubles in size when cooked, so it takes two cups water plus one cup raw rice to make four servings of one-half cup each. Instant rice is prepared with one cup water per cup of rice. A cup of instant rice makes a cup of cooked rice. Ready-to-eat rice is also sold in shelf-stable tubs and pouches, and specialty stores sell canned, cooked rice mixtures such as rice and beans, Spanish rice, or wild rice. In these recipes, rice means raw rice that has been picked over, rinsed, and drained.

ALMOND RICE

SERVES 6–8

       3¾ cups water

       Small can crushed pineapple, with juice

       2 cups long-grain white rice

       1 teaspoon almond extract

       Salt and pepper to taste

       Sliced, toasted almonds to taste

Bring water and undrained pineapple to a boil and stir in rice. Cover, reduce heat, and cook over low heat 20 minutes without peeking. Stir in extract. Adjust seasonings. Serve sprinkled with sliced almonds. Makes 6 to 8 side dish servings.

SUNNY-SIDE RICE ALFREDO

SERVES 6

> 8- to 10-ounce jar of marinated artichoke hearts
>
> 15-ounce can yellow vegetable such as whole kernel corn, sliced wax beans, or diced carrots
>
> 15-ounce jar of Alfredo sauce
>
> 3 cups cooked rice
>
> 1 teaspoon turmeric

Drain artichoke hearts and chop. Drain canned vegetable and discard juice or save it for another purpose. Place artichokes, vegetable, rice, turmeric, and Alfredo sauce in a pan. Heat gently until heated through.

Cook's note: To make this a main dish, add drained and rinsed garbanzo beans, diced ham, or chopped, cooked egg.

A good supply of aluminum foil lets you cook on an open fire or jury-rig a solar oven.
(Reynolds)

NUTTER-ITIOUS RICE

SERVES 6

By using brown rice and plenty of protein-rich, low-fat nuts you create a vegan main dish or a rich side dish.

> 1½ cups brown rice
>
> 2 tablespoons olive oil
>
> 3 cups water
>
> 3 bouillon cubes (chicken, beef, or vegetable)
>
> 15-ounce can peas and diced carrots, drained
>
> ¼ cup each sliced almonds, sunflower "nuts," and coarsely chopped walnuts
>
> Salt and pepper to taste

Sizzle rice in hot olive oil to coat well. Add water and bouillon and bring to a boil. Cook rice until tender. Fold in carrots and nuts. Adjust seasonings and serve hot, at room temperature, or chilled. Makes 6 portions as a side dish or serves 3 as a vegan main dish.

BULGUR RICE PILAF

SERVES 4–6

Mixing two starches, such as bulgur and rice, makes for a more interesting shelf meal. Add meat and vegetables if you wish to make it a main dish.

> ¼ cup liquid such as water, tea, broth, wine, juice
>
> ⅓ cup diced dried onion bits
>
> ⅓ cup canola oil
>
> 1 cup raw rice
>
> 4 cups water
>
> 4 teaspoons bouillon or base (chicken, beef, or vegetable)
>
> ¾ cup bulgur
>
> 2 or more cups cooked or canned vegetables, meat, eggs, or seafood (optional)

Soak onion bits in ¼ cup liquid. Heat oil and stir in rice to coat. Add softened, drained onions. Add water, bring to a boil, and stir in bouillon and rice. Cover and cook over low heat 20 minutes or until rice is tender. Remove from heat. Stir in bulgur and let stand, covered in a warm place, 20 minutes until bulgur absorbs water and is tender. Fluff and serve.

To eat as a main dish, stir in additional ingredients and return to low heat to heat through. Season to taste.

PINEAPPLE NUT STUFFING

SERVES 6

Serve this stuffing with canned ham or Spam or add an extra egg and more nuts to make it a vegetarian main dish.

> 4 cups dry bread cubes or unflavored croutons
>
> Small can crushed pineapple with juice
>
> Water
>
> ½ cup broken walnuts or pecans
>
> 2 eggs or equivalent in reconstituted eggs
>
> ¼ cup olive oil

Mix bread, pineapple with its juice, and walnuts. Whisk eggs with oil and fold into bread mixture. Stir in enough water to form a moist dressing. Bake in a buttered pan at 350°F until it's toasty and "set." If fresh eggs are used, internal temperature should register a minimum of 160°F. Serves 6 as a side dish or 4 as a main dish. This recipe can also be baked in a stove-top oven, covered grill, or solar cooker.

SESAME GREEN BEANS

SERVES 4

> 2 cans, 14.5 ounces each, French-cut green beans
>
> 2 tablespoon dried onion flakes
>
> 2 tablespoons dried celery flakes
>
> 2 tablespoons olive oil
>
> ¼ cup sliced almonds (or more to taste)
>
> 2 tablespoons black sesame seeds (or more to taste)
>
> Freshly ground pepper to taste

Drain green beans into the dried onion and celery and let them soak in the juice 10 to 15 minutes. Drain. Heat olive oil and stir in almonds, sesame seeds, onion, and celery until fragrant. Fold in green beans, cover, and cook over low heat. Serves 4 as a side dish, 2 as a vegetarian main dish.

GREEN RICE

SERVES 8

> ¼ cup extra virgin olive oil
>
> 2 cups long-grain rice
>
> 4 cups water
>
> 4 bouillon cubes (chicken, beef, vegetable)
>
> 3 to 4 tablespoons sweet bell pepper flakes
>
> 2 tablespoons dried onion bits
>
> 2 tablespoons freeze-dried chives
>
> 4 tablespoons dried parsley flakes
>
> ¼ cup freeze-dried English peas

In a saucepan or pressure cooker, stir rice into hot oil until well coated. Add water, bouillon, and the green pepper, onion, and parsley flakes. Bring to a boil and stir to dissolve bouillon. Add peas. Bring to a boil . Cook one minute under pressure or 20 minutes, covered, over low heat. Makes 8 servings of ½ cup each.

Cook's note: Bouillon is salty. Don't add salt without tasting. Add pepper to taste.

CREAMY CHEESE GRITS

SERVES 4

The creamiest of grits, this side dish can be topped with almost any meat or vegetable to make a colorful meal.

¼ cup water

2 tablespoons dried garlic granules

1½ cups water

1 chicken, ham, or vegetable bouillon cube

½ cup yellow or white stone-ground grits

½ cup tinned cream

⅓ cup grated Parmesan

In a medium saucepan, soak garlic in water for 10 minutes or so. Stir in 1½ cups water. Bring to a boil and stir in bouillon cube and grits. Stir over medium heat until thick. Stir in cream until grits are thick and creamy. Remove from heat and fold in cheese.

NO-COOK POTATO SALAD

SERVES 6

This is as close as we can come to a passable potato salad without fresh vegetables or hard-cooked eggs. No cooking required.

15-ounce can of potatoes, drained and rinsed

15-ounce can of mixed vegetables such as Veg-All, drained

Small can of diced water chestnuts, drained and rinsed

Small jar of diced pimentos, drained

Small can of sliced ripe olives, drained (optional)

Bottled ranch or other creamy salad dressing

Dried chives or parsley

Cut potatoes into bite size and toss lightly with vegetables, water chestnuts, pimentos, olives. and dressing to taste. Sprinkle with dried chives or parsley.

ORCHARD SKILLET

SERVES 6

When the menu cries out for a side dish with fruity tang and texture, try this recipe. It's especially good with pork and poultry dishes. Crumbled thyme is preferable to powdered. Be sure to use pie-sliced apples, not apple pie filling.

>   ¼ cup olive oil
>
>   1 teaspoon each onion powder, dried parsley
>
>   2 teaspoons dried, crumbled thyme
>
>   ¼ cup brown sugar
>
>   2 tablespoons cider vinegar
>
>   2 cans, 15 ounces each, pie-sliced apples, undrained

Heat the olive oil. Stir in onion powder, parsley, thyme, and brown sugar over low heat. Stir in vinegar. Fold in apples until they are thoroughly coated with the butter-herb mixture and heated through. Serves 6 as a side dish.

COPPER CARROT COINS

Since Grandmother's time, this potluck classic has been made in a huge batch that requires a can of condensed cream of tomato soup. Here's a smaller version.

>   15-ounce can sliced carrots
>
>   1 packet instant cream of tomato soup
>
>   ½ cup hot water
>
>   1 tablespoon olive oil
>
>   2 tablespoons apple cider vinegar
>
>   2 tablespoons brown sugar

Drain carrots. In a bowl mix tomato soup and hot water. Stir in oil, vinegar, and sugar until sugar dissolves. Fold in carrots. Serve warm, at room temperature, or chilled.

MAPLE MUSTARD HARICOTS VERTS

SERVES 6–8

>   2 to 3 cans whole green beans
>
>   3 tablespoons maple syrup or maple-flavored pancake syrup
>
>   2 tablespoons grainy mustard
>
>   1 tablespoon each balsamic vinegar, olive oil

While beans heat in their juice, whisk remaining ingredients together. Drain beans, drizzle with sauce, and mix gently. Serve hot.

RED CABBAGE SLAW

SERVES 6

This can be made in two quite different versions. Make it with fennel seed this time and caraway seed next time.

>   1 tablespoon fennel seeds OR 1 tablespoon caraway seeds
>
>   ¼ cup olive oil
>
>   24-ounce jar of sweet 'n sour red cabbage
>
>   ¼ cup dried cranberries, raisins, or currants
>
>   Sugar or vinegar to taste

In a heavy saucepan or skillet, heat seeds over high heat just until fragrant. Stir in olive oil, cabbage, and dried fruit. Heat through and adjust seasoning.

HARVARD BEETS

SERVES 6

Beets come in jars or cans and can be whole, diced, julienne, or sliced. They are one of the most versatile vegetables in the prepared pantry because they can be served hot and buttered, pickled, cold in salads, or in this tangy sauce. Harvard Beets are traditionally diced. If yours are larger, chop them coarsely.

> 2 cans, 15 ounces each, beets
>
> ⅓ cup sugar or equivalent
>
> ⅛ teaspoon ground cloves
>
> 1 tablespoon cornstarch
>
> ⅔ cup beet juice
>
> ¼ cup tarragon vinegar

Drain beets, saving ⅔ cup juice. In a cold saucepan mix sugar, cloves, cornstarch, the ⅔ cup beet juice, and vinegar. Heat, stirring, over medium heat until it thickens. Reduce heat, stir in beets, cover, and cook until beets are heated through.

More Side Dish Inspirations

All of these can be made from your pantry shelf in ways that add new life to the bland and canned.

Dilly Carrots: Heat one or two cans of baby carrots in their juice. When they're thoroughly hot, drain well and stir in a tablespoon or two of olive oil, a teaspoon of dillweed, and freshly ground pepper to taste. Stir and serve.

Peas with Mushrooms: Drain mushrooms and swizzle in a saucepan with a little hot vegetable oil. When mushrooms are toasty brown, stir in drained peas, a little dried thyme, and a small jar of drained, diced pimento. Heat gently and serve.

Tarragon Green Beans: Heat two cans of kitchen-sliced green beans until hot, then drain and stir in a drizzle of vegetable oil and a drift of dried tarragon.

Potatoes in Caraway Sauce: Heat a thin layer of vegetable oil in a skillet and stir-fry drained, canned potatoes until browned. Stir in caraway seeds to taste.

Stewed Tomatoes: Heat a can of diced tomatoes with juice until boiling. Turn off heat and stir in herbed croutons to taste. Sprinkle with grated Romano or Parmesan and serve at once.

Cook's note: French-fried onions from the shelf add interest, texture, and taste to canned vegetables. Use sparingly and toss with hot vegetables to taste.

Sauces Save the Meal

When you are relying on shelf meals, the added sass of a sauce can turn blah to *bellissimo!*

Sauces are so crucial to classic cuisine that a double boiler or bain marie is a must in French kitchens. If you don't have room for extra pots, use low heat and a deft touch to keep sauces from curdling or burning.

Follow directions carefully, be patient, stir constantly, and use a flame spreader if necessary to keep heat very low, especially when cooking any milk-based sauce.

APRICOT SAUCE

> 8- to 10-ounce jar apricot jam
>
> ½ teaspoon ground ginger (or more to taste)
>
> About ¼ cup apricot liqueur, apricot nectar, or strongly brewed peach tea

Heat jam gently and stir in ginger and enough liquid to make a spoon-able sauce. Serve over ham, chicken, rice pilaf, crepes, or sweet potatoes.

TOMATO SOUP SAUCE

> 1 can condensed tomato soup
>
> 1 tablespoon grainy mustard
>
> ⅓ cup apple cider vinegar
>
> ¾ cup packed brown sugar

Heat gently, stirring everything together until sugar dissolves. Serve warm on pork, chicken, sausage, ham loaf, omelet, vegetables.

SWEET AND SOUR SAUCE

> 1 cup vegetable oil
>
> ¾ cup sugar
>
> ¼ cup raspberry vinegar
>
> ⅓ cup ketchup
>
> 1 tablespoon Worcestershire sauce

Stir or shake everything together until sugar dissolves. Let stand 30 minutes or more while flavors marry. Spoon to taste over hot or cold vegetables.

PINEAPPLE SAUCE

The natural sweetness of pineapple is enough for some tastes. For a sweeter sauce add sugar and/or raisins. Spoon this sauce over canned ham, fried Spam, or chicken croquettes.

> Small can of crushed pineapple
>
> Water
>
> 2 tablespoons cornstarch
>
> 1½ teaspoons dry mustard
>
> ¼ cup sugar (optional)
>
> ¼ cup raisins (optional)
>
> 2 tablespoons soy sauce

Drain the pineapple into a measuring cup and add water to make 1 cup. Add this liquid to a cold saucepan and stir in cornstarch and dry mustard. Stir over low heat while adding pineapple, raisins, sugar, and soy sauce. Heat, stirring, until sauce thickens. Makes about 2 cups.

HOT FUDGE SAUCE

Turn almost anything into a celebration sweet when you slather it with fudge sauce. Spoon this sauce warm over any cake, broken cookies, pudding, fresh or canned, fruit or marshmallows melted over the campfire.

> 12-ounce bag of dark chocolate chips
>
> 12-ounce can of evaporated milk
>
> ½ to 1 cup sugar
>
> 1 teaspoon each vanilla extract and butter flavoring

In a heavy saucepan over low heat or in a double boiler over steaming water, melt chocolate in the milk. Stir in sugar to dissolve it. Stir in flavorings. Serve warm. Makes about 2 cups.

QUICKSTEP CARAMEL FROSTING

This delicious goo covers any cake, cookies, or fruit to complete a boffo dessert.

> 1 can sweetened condensed milk
>
> ¼ cup packed brown sugar
>
> ½ stick butter (¼ cup)
>
> ½ teaspoon vanilla extract
>
> ¾ cup flaked coconut (optional)
>
> ¾ cup chopped, roasted pecans (optional)

Use a heavy pan over low flame and bring everything to a boil, stirring constantly 3 to 5 minutes. Remove from heat and stir in coconut, nuts, or both. Makes 2 to 3 cups.

BALSAMIC MUSTARD SAUCE

> 3 tablespoons each olive oil and flour
>
> 1 tablespoon dry mustard powder
>
> Pinch salt, pepper
>
> 12-ounce can of evaporated milk
>
> Water
>
> 2 tablespoons balsamic vinegar

In a cold saucepan stir oil, flour, mustard powder, salt, and pepper. Add enough water to the canned milk to make 1½ cups and whisk into dry ingredients. Heat, stirring over low fire, until the mixture thickens. Remove from heat and stir in balsamic vinegar. If a thinner sauce is desired, stir in water one teaspoon at a time. Serve warm over meat, game, vegetables, casseroles, egg dishes.

BLACKBERRY KETCHUP

Whip up this "ketchup" to add color and a daring flash of flavor to anything from meats and fish to scrambled eggs. Spoon it on grilled tofu. Use it as a dipping sauce with chunks of pita or peasant bread. Use it sparingly over reconstituted strawberries or canned peaches.

> 10-ounce jar of seedless blackberry preserves
>
> ⅓ cup each water, apple cider vinegar, and brown sugar
>
> 1½ teaspoons apple pie spice or pumpkin pie spice
>
> ¼ teaspoon cayenne pepper (optional)

In a saucepan heat everything together, stirring until preserves melt and sugar dissolves. Boil 3 minutes. Keeps up to two weeks in the refrigerator. Use it warm or cold.

BALSAMIC DRIZZLE

This all-purpose sauce is used with a very light touch over meat, vegetables, fruit, omelets, or bruschetta.

> 1½ cups balsamic vinegar
>
> ¼ cup packed brown sugar
>
> ⅓ cup honey

Combine ingredients and bring to a low boil for 8 to 10 minutes. Use sparingly.

MUSHROOM-MATO SAUCE

SERVES 6

The marketplace offers so many types of dried mushrooms, the creative cook will have several varieties on hand to keep meals interesting and varied. If you use fresh or canned mushrooms you'll need 2 cups.

> 1 cup dried mushrooms
>
> 1 tablespoon dried onion bits
>
> 1 tablespoon canola or olive oil
>
> 1 teaspoon garlic powder or granules (not garlic salt)
>
> 28- to 32-ounce can crushed tomatoes
>
> 1 tablespoon mixed Italian seasoning
>
> Freshly ground pepper to taste

Combine mushrooms and dried onions. Reconstitute them according to directions for the mushrooms. In a saucepan combine mushrooms, onions, olive oil, garlic, tomatoes, and herbs. Simmer until mushrooms are tender. Add pepper to taste. This is enough sauce for 6 servings of pasta, or spoon the sauce over meat, seafood, toast, or vegetables.

ALFREDO SAUCE LITE

SERVES 6

In the pantry, jars of shelf-stable Parmesan cheese are a lifesaver. This recipe uses an entire 8-ounce jar.

>   2 tablespoons flour
>
>   2 tablespoons olive oil
>
>   About 3 cups reconstituted fat-free milk
>
>   1 cup grated regular or "lite" Parmesan cheese

In a large, nonstick skillet stir flour into warm olive oil and keep stirring over low heat while you slowly add 2½ cups milk. When it thickens, remove from heat and stir in cheese. Add more milk little by little to make the desired consistency of sauce. This is enough sauce for 6 servings of cooked linguini. Toss with cooked pasta or spoon over vegetables, tofu, or an omelet. Pass the pepper mill.

Chapter 10

Desperation Desserts

Desserts become more important than ever when you're relying on pantry foods during an emergency, a long journey, or a long winter in a remote cabin. The more difficult the day, the more important these little rewards become. See the Appendix for baking without an oven.

OLIVE OIL CAKE

This rich and satisfying sweet is mixed with a whisk, no mixer required. Experiment with different combinations of extracts such as vanilla and rum, cherry and almond, orange and lemon.

> 1½ cups flour
>
> 1 teaspoon baking powder
>
> ½ teaspoon baking soda
>
> Pinch salt
>
> ⅔ cup sugar
>
> ⅔ cup olive oil
>
> 3 eggs or equivalent
>
> ½ cup water or fruit juice
>
> 1½ teaspoons orange, vanilla, almond, or lemon extract

Put dry ingredients in a clean plastic bag and "work" the bag gently to mix. Whisk wet ingredients together until well blended, then whisk in dry ingredients until everything is evenly moistened. Do not overbeat. Put in a greased baking pan or pans no more than ⅔ full. Bake at 350°F about 30 minutes or until the cake is firm and pulling slightly away from the pan. Serve as is or with a sauce or a sprinkling of powdered sugar.

SHOO FLY CAKE

SERVES 6–8

This cake version of Shoo Fly Pie is easy to make without a beater and it makes its own topping.

> 2 cups flour
>
> 1 cup brown sugar
>
> ¾ stick of butter or butter-flavor shortening
>
> 1 cup boiling water
>
> ½ cup molasses
>
> 1½ teaspoons baking soda

Cut butter or shortening into a mixture of the flour and brown sugar until mealy. Remove and save a heaping half cup of the mixture. Bring water to a boil in a pan large enough to hold at least 3 cups. (Mixture will froth up.) Stir molasses and baking soda into hot water until it stops foaming, then fold liquid into the flour mixture until it's evenly moistened. Put in a greased pan and sprinkle with reserved crumb mixture. Bake at 350°F for 40 to 45 minutes or until it's springy to the touch. Serve as is or with vanilla sauce.

APPLE BROWN BETTY

SERVES 6–8

> 1½ cups crumbled cinnamon graham crackers OR 1½ cups graham cracker crumbs mixed with 1 teaspoon ground cinnamon
>
> 2 cans of apple pie filling OR 2 cans of pie-sliced apples plus sweeteners and a tablespoon of apple pie spices
>
> ⅓ cup vegetable oil
>
> ⅓ cup butterscotch flavored baking chips

To make cracker crumbs, place them in a freezer bag and roll with a rolling pin or round bottle. Grease a baking pan and add apples. Sprinkle apples evenly with crumbs and drizzle with oil. Sprinkle butterscotch chips on top. Bake at 375°F until chips melt and crumbs form a golden crust.

stove-top method: Heat apples over low fire in a heavy covered pan or skillet. Stir in butterscotch chips, take off the burner, and stir to melt chips. Cover and set aside. In a nonstick skillet, stir oil and crumbs together over medium heat until they are toasty. Spoon over hot apple mixture and serve at once.

APPLESAUCE SKILLET CAKE

SERVES 8–10

This makes a large, moist cake that requires slow cooking for even baking atop the stove.

> 4 eggs or equivalent
>
> ¼ cup vegetable oil
>
> 1½ cups sugar
>
> 1 teaspoon vanilla
>
> 1⅔ cups applesauce
>
> 12-ounce can baby carrots
>
> 2¼ cups flour
>
> 1 tablespoon baking soda
>
> 1 teaspoon salt
>
> 1 tablespoon cinnamon
>
> 1 teaspoon nutmeg
>
> 1 cup raisins
>
> ½ cup chopped nuts

Grease a cold, deep, 10-inch cast aluminum skillet. In a large bowl whisk eggs and oil, gradually adding sugar. Add vanilla and applesauce. Drain carrots very well, chop finely, and add to egg mixture. Mix dry ingredients in a bag, then dump into wet ingredients and fold in until everything is evenly moistened. Fold in nuts and raisins. Spread in a cold skillet, cover tightly, and place over medium-low burner for 30 minutes. Then check for doneness every 5 minutes.

Cake should be springy to the touch and slightly pulling away from sides of the skillet. Don't be tempted to turn heat higher or remove the lid too often. When cake is done, let it cool in the skillet, uncovered. Cut in wedges. Serve plain or with tinned cream, vanilla sauce, or a sprinkling of powdered sugar.

STRAWBERRY CHEWS

SERVES 8–10

> 1 box of strawberry-flavored cake mix
>
> 1½ cups vegetable oil
>
> 2½ cups rolled oats
>
> 12-ounce jar of strawberry jam
>
> 2 tablespoons water or strawberry schnapps

Set the oven to 350°F. Blend cake mix, oil, and rolled oats in a bowl until crumbly. Press half the mixture into a sprayed 9 x 13-inch baking pan and put in the hot oven for 5 minutes. In a small pan, gently heat jam just until it's soft enough to stir in the water or liqueur. Spread jam over bottom crust and sprinkle with remaining crumbs. Bake 20 to 25 minutes more until golden brown. Let cool, then cut in squares.

FORBIDDEN FRUIT RICE PUDDING

SERVES 8–10

If you make a smaller version of this recipe, don't use the entire can of condensed milk. It's just too sweet.

> Small can crushed pineapple
>
> 1 teaspoon almond extract
>
> 4 cups cooked rice
>
> ½ cup golden raisins
>
> ½ cup shredded coconut
>
> 13-ounce can sweetened condensed milk

Open the can of pineapple and mix in the almond extract. Fold together pineapple, rice, raisins, and coconut with condensed milk to taste. Serves 8 to 10 for dessert, 4 to 5 as a breakfast main dish.

HOMEMADE HALVAH

SERVES 10–12

A traditional Mediterranean fudge is made from ingredients that keep well on a shelf. When you need a nutritious, satisfying candy here's a good one to try.

> 12- to 16-ounce can or jar of tahini (sesame paste)
>
> The same amount of honey—12 ounces is 1½ cups; 16 ounces is 2 cups
>
> An equal amount of finely chopped nuts (more or less to taste)

In a heavy saucepan over low-medium heat, warm the honey just until little bubbles begin to form around the edge. Remove from heat and whisk tahini into honey by the tablespoon until it's smooth. Fold in chopped nuts. Spread in a sprayed dish or pan and let cool and set for 24 to 48 hours. Mixture will be firmer if refrigerated. Serve in squares or, if it's not firm enough, eat it with a spoon or use it as a spread.

BUTTERSCOTCH POPCORN

Unlike recipes that require long boiling to bring syrup to the "soft ball stage," this recipe has less guesswork. You do need a way to bake it, but a solar or reflector oven or covered grill will do the job.

> 16 cups popped corn without salt or oil
>
> 1½ cups nuts (optional)
>
> 1¼ cups packed brown sugar
>
> ½ cup butter or butter-flavor shortening
>
> ½ cup light corn syrup
>
> ½ teaspoon salt
>
> 1 teaspoon vanilla, butter-rum, or rum extract
>
> ¼ teaspoon baking soda

Put popcorn (and nuts if using them) in greased baking pan(s). Set the oven for 250°F. Bring sugar, butter, corn syrup, salt, and flavoring to a boil, stirring constantly. When it boils, reduce heat and keep at a low boil for five minutes by the clock. Turn off heat and stir in baking soda. Use a sprayed spatula to keep mixing gently as you slowly pour the syrup over the popcorn. Spread in pan(s) and bake 50 to 60 minutes, stirring every 15 minutes. Spread on parchment or waxed paper to cool, then break in chunks for a dessert to heat by the handful.

FRY-PAN COOKIES

SERVES 4–6

> 1 cup each sugar and flour
>
> 1 teaspoon baking powder
>
> 3 eggs or equivalent
>
> 1 teaspoon vanilla extract
>
> 1½ cups chopped, pitted dates
>
> 1 cup chopped nuts
>
> Confectioners sugar

Grease a heavy 10-inch skillet (preferably cast aluminum) generously with butter or solid shortening. Put flour, sugar, and baking powder in a clean bag to mix. In a bowl, beat eggs well and dump in flour mixture. Stir to mix, then fold in dates and nuts. Batter will be very stiff.

Spread batter in the cold skillet, cover tightly, and place over low-medium heat 20 to 30 minutes or until firm and pulling slightly away from the edges of the pan. Stove-top baking takes practice, depending on your burners and type of pans. Strive for even heat and peek as little as possible.

Let pan cool for 10 to 15 minutes. Sprinkle with powdered sugar. Cut in wedges and dredge in more sugar as you remove each wedge to a serving plate or cookie jar.

MINCEMEAT CREAM

SERVES 12–16

Mincemeat is available all year in most supermarkets and featured during November and December. Although mincemeat pie has fallen out of fashion in recent years, mincemeat itself is a sweet, spicy, versatile ingredient that keeps on the pantry shelf for months.

> 28-ounce jar mincemeat
>
> 2 tablespoons brandy or rum (optional)
>
> 2 tablespoons each brown sugar, flour
>
> 14-ounce can of tinned cream
>
> 1 cup coarsely chopped nuts

Spray or butter a baking pan and spread mincemeat in it. Sprinkle with spirits if using. Mix sugar and flour with cream and spread over mincemeat. Sprinkle nuts on top. Bake 40 to 45 minutes at 325°F and serve warm or at room temperature. It's very rich, so serve it in very small portions. Serve as is or spoon it sparingly over ham, hot or cold breakfast cereal, stewed apples, or plain pudding or cake.

ROAD RUBBLE PIE

SERVES 8–10

Pecan meal is sold in supermarkets. Packaged graham cracker crumbs can be used, or make your own by putting graham crackers in a freezer bag and rolling them with a rolling pin or bottle. This also bakes well with the indirect baking method using a pie tin inside a Dutch oven.

> 1 stick butter or butter-flavored shortening
>
> 1 teaspoon sugar
>
> About 1¼ cups flour
>
> 4 eggs or equivalent
>
> 1 cup sugar
>
> 1 teaspoon vanilla
>
> 1½ cups pecan meal
>
> 1½ cups graham cracker crumbs
>
> 1½ cups shredded coconut

While the oven preheats to 325°F, melt butter or shortening. Mix melted butter, flour, and sugar in the pie pan and use floured fingers to press it evenly over the bottom and sides of the pan to form a crust. Flute edges. Set aside. Whisk together the eggs, sugar, and vanilla, then fold in the pecan meal, cracker crumbs, and coconut. Fill the pie shell and bake 35 to 40 minutes or until the filling is set and the crust golden brown. Cool completely before cutting. It's rich, so make slices small.

Grill or pan-brown a canned peach half and fill it with cream for an elegant fruit course.

CAKE-MIX COOKIES

MAKES ABOUT 4 DOZEN COOKIES

Make these cookies with almost any flavor of regular cake mix. Make them different each time with different combinations: chocolate cake mix with chopped pecans, spice cake mix with pistachios, orange flavored cake mix with golden raisins, and so on.

> 2 eggs or equivalent in reconstituted eggs
>
> 1 cup canola or corn oil
>
> 1 box of cake mix (2-layer size)
>
> 1 cup one-minute rolled oats
>
> 1 cup raisins, chocolate chips, dried cranberries, chopped nuts, etc.

Set the oven for 375°F. Beat eggs and beat in oil. Stir in cake mix, then fold in oats and the addition of your choice. Drop by tablespoons, allowing room for cookies to spread, on baking sheets lined with nonstick foil or parchment. Bake 10 to 12 minutes or until cookies are firm.

Bar cookies: Spread dough in a 9 x 13-inch baking dish and bake 35 to 45 minutes or until firm. Cool and cut into squares.

skillet cookies: Grease a heavy, 10- or 12-inch skillet. Spread dough evenly, cover, and cook over low flame, with flame spreader if necessary, until firm. Cool and cut in wedges. For a thinner cookie use two skillets.

AMBROSIA

SERVES 10

This recipe works the same whether you use sugar-free or regular pudding mix. Fruits may be canned in their own juice or in "lite" syrup. It's best with canned fruit, not rehydrated fruit. Avoid fruits canned in heavy syrup.

>5 pitted dried plums, cut up, or ½ cup raisins
>
>½ cup rum, sweet wine, or fruit juice
>
>*Four cans of fruit, such as:*
>
>>15-ounce can apricot halves
>>
>>15-ounce can pitted sweet cherries
>>
>>15-ounce can diced peaches
>>
>>15-ounce can diced pears
>>
>>20-ounce can pineapple tidbits or crushed pineapple
>>
>>12-ounce can tropical blend fruit
>>
>>15-ounce can lychees
>
>4-serving package instant French vanilla pudding
>
>½ cup shredded coconut (optional)

Heat rum, wine, or juice, and pour over dried plums or raisins. Cover loosely and set aside to cool and get plump. Choose any four cans of fruit, drain cans, and reserve 1¾ cups juice. Whisk juice and pudding mix together until well mixed and fold in drained fruit and coconut. Spoon into serving dishes. Serve at once or chill.

DUMP CAKE YOUR WAY

SERVES 12–15

Dump" cakes have been around for generations. Today the ingredients still belong on the pantry shelf for a jiffy dessert. Mix and match for a different treat each time. Other variations might include butterscotch chips instead of nuts, raisins instead of coconut, and so on. To make a Black Forest version, use chocolate cake mix, chocolate chips, and cherry pie filling.

> 1 can peach, blueberry, strawberry, cherry, or apple pie filling
>
> 20-ounce can crushed pineapple or tidbits packed in their own juice
>
> 2-layer size box of white, yellow, French vanilla, orange, spice, strawberry, or lemon cake mix
>
> 1 cup each shredded coconut, chopped nuts
>
> 1¼ cups vegetable oil

Grease a 9 x 13-inch baking pan. Set the oven to 325°F. Spread pie filling in the bottom, then add an even layer of pineapple with its juice. Sprinkle with cake mix, coconut, and nuts. Drizzle evenly and thoroughly with oil. Bake 60 to 75 minutes or until toasty.

FLAN

SERVES 6

Canned *dulce de leche* is already caramelized, a huge shortcut in recipes. Find it in the Hispanic food aisle. Custards are best baked in a water bath, so this recipe isn't recommended for cooking in a boat underway.

> 14-ounce can dulce de leche
>
> ⅓ cup water
>
> ½ cup sugar
>
> 2 cups milk
>
> 5 eggs or equivalent
>
> 1 teaspoon vanilla extract

Set the oven to 350°F. In a pan over low heat stir dulce de leche, water, and sugar until sugar dissolves and liquid is smooth. Remove from heat. Butter half a dozen custard cups or a 1½-quart baking dish and set it in a shallow pan with an inch of water. Whisk milk, eggs, and vanilla into the dulce de leche mixture. Pour into prepared containers and bake 25 minutes or until custard "sets." Taking every precaution, discard hot water and let custard cool.

Chapter 11

Snacks and Trail Mix

Snacks in a Sack

During good times and bad there are solid reasons to snack on healthful foods that fit in a pocket or backpack. These recipes are assembled in a big batch and are easily divided into smaller packages for the lunch box, carry-on bag, or briefcase. If you keep one sweet and one savory gorp on hand you're ready anytime to take breakfast on a fitness walk, grab a packet for airline travel, stand night watch on the boat, or leave the supper table to nibble dessert while taking a twilight stroll.

If you're health conscious or have allergies, ingredients here can be substituted as long as proportions remain the same. You might, for example, use soy nuts instead of tree nuts, or make sure dried fruits are unsulphured, or use noncaloric sweeteners.

Many of these recipes are also useful as sprinkles over salads, vegetables, or plain pudding. They add flavor and crunch to bland shelf meals.

Water is the first essential, so bring plenty of liquids to wash down these trail mixes.

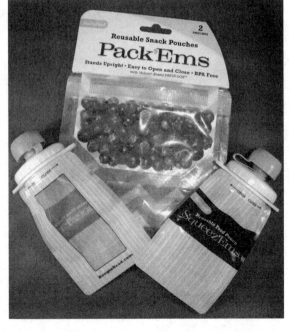

Refillable tubes and reusable snack bags are ideal for backpacking and for carrying healthful snacks in your pocket or day pack.

SUGARPLUM GORP

MAKES 14–15 CUPS

Don't wait for Christmas to make this nourishing dessert gorp. Dried dates and plums are excellent keepers in the ample pantry.

12-ounce package diced, pitted dates

12-ounce package moist dried plums, cut up

½ teaspoon ground nutmeg

⅛ teaspoon ground cloves

2 teaspoons cinnamon

1 cup coarse natural (raw) sugar

12 cups popcorn, popped without salt or oil

Put fruit in a big bag or clean container. Mix spices and sugar and toss with dried fruit to coat. Add popcorn and toss lightly to mix well. Serve in bowls or package it in individual snack bags. Keep cool and dry.

CREOLE GORP

MAKES 15 CUPS

This kicky trail mix can be made with totally gluten-free ingredients. Read labels to be sure. Watch the heat! Cajun seasoning and Tabasco both pack a wallop.

½ cup corn oil or other vegetable oil

1 tablespoon butter-flavored popcorn salt

1 to 2 tablespoons Cajun seasoning

4 drops Tabasco

10 cups plain popcorn

2 cups parched corn (ready-to-eat snack food)

2 cups peanuts, regular or hot 'n spicy

1 cup whole almonds or pecans, unsalted

Whisk oil with popcorn salt and Cajun seasoning. Put popcorn in a big bowl or clean dish pan and drizzle with oil mixture. Mix well. Lightly stir in parched corn and nuts. Spread mixture in two 9 x 13-inch baking pans and bake 10 minutes at 350°F. Stir and bake another few minutes until flavors have penetrated. Cool completely. Serve in a big bowl or package the mix by the cupful for the trail.

WHITEOUT GORP

MAKES 18 CUPS

White-on-white sets the scene for a snack that's good indoors and out. It's an ideal dessert to eat on the go.

> ½ cup powdered sugar
>
> 12 cups plain popcorn (no butter, no salt)
>
> 2 cups shredded coconut
>
> 2 cups white yogurt-covered raisins
>
> 2 cups blanched almonds

Put the popcorn and powdered sugar in a large, clean bag and shake it gently to coat the popcorn. Add other ingredients and shake gently to mix. Serve in bowls or measure the mix into packages by the cupful. Makes 18 one-cup portions.

DATING GAME GORP

MAKES 48 PIECES

> 24 whole, pitted dates
>
> 24 dried apricots or dried plums
>
> 48 whole almonds, pecans, or hazelnuts
>
> 1 packet flavored gelatin dessert mix (orange is good)

Force a whole nut into each pitted date. Cut a small pocket in each apricot or plum and slip a nut into each. Put stuffed pieces in a bag with dry dessert mix and shake gently to coat. Package in snack bags.

Measuring homemade trail mixes into individual containers keeps them fresh and gives you portion control.

FIERY FRUITCAKE GORP

MAKES 16 HALF-CUP PORTIONS

This recipe calls for ready-to-eat dried fruit, not the rock-hard dehydrated fruits sold for the survival pantry.

> ¼ cup olive oil
>
> 1 teaspoon bottled hot sauce (or more if you like more heat)
>
> 1 tablespoon chili powder
>
> 1 teaspoon each salt, pepper
>
> 4 cups unsalted whole almonds
>
> 4 cups dried fruit such as apricots or raisins

In a large, heavy skillet, heat olive oil and stir in hot sauce, chili powder, salt, and pepper. Stir in almonds and stir-fry to coat well. Let cool completely. Cut up large pieces of dried fruit such as apricots and prunes. Mix in nuts. Package in individual servings and keep in a cool place for up to a week.

DAY AT THE ZOO GORP

MAKES 14 CUPS

Animal crackers are low in fat and sugar compared to many cookies. This snack is fun for kids and it also has enough carbs to turbocharge a hike, bike ride, or climb.

> 2 cups fish-shaped gummi candy
>
> ½ cup coarse sugar such as Sugar in the Raw
>
> 4 cups animal crackers
>
> 2 cups whole-grain goldfish crackers
>
> 2 cups oyster crackers, preferably low sodium
>
> 4 cups mixed nuts, preferably unsalted

Put gummi candy and sugar in a bag and mix gently to coat any sticky places on the candy. Add remaining ingredients and mix gently. Package by the cup or half cup in snack bags for the trail.

ASIAN OCCASION POPCORN

MAKES 7 HALF-CUP PORTIONS

Popcorn is one of the prepper's most important supplies. Here's a different way to use it in trail mix.

> 4 cups popcorn, popped without salt or oil
>
> 2 cups crisp Chinese noodles
>
> 1 cup hot 'n spicy roasted peanuts
>
> 1 teaspoon Tabasco sauce
>
> 1 tablespoon dark sesame oil

Spread popcorn, noodles, and nuts on a paper or in a pan. Drizzle very slowly with a mixture of the oil and Tabasco, tossing and mixing constantly.

WOODSMOKE GORP

MAKES 12 CUPS

This hearty gorp can see you through a predawn watch in a duck blind or get you to the top of that yonder peak.

> 2 cups whole walnut halves
>
> 2 teaspoons hickory smoked salt
>
> 8 cups unsalted plain popcorn
>
> ¼ cup olive oil
>
> 8-ounce container of grated Parmesan cheese
>
> 2 cups low-sodium turkey jerky cut in bite-sized pieces

Put nuts, salt, and popcorn in a large, clean bag and shake gently to mix thoroughly. Drizzle with olive oil and mix again. Add cheese, shake again, then add jerky and shake one more time. Serve in a big bowl or package by the cupful for the trail.

GARLIC LOVER'S GORP

MAKES 12 CUPS

Keep vampires away with this garlicky trail mix when you hike, climb, or camp out. The dried parsley, some believe, will keep you from having garlic breath. However, this pungent mix isn't recommended for airline passengers.

- 4 cups garlic croutons
- 16-ounce package garlic summer sausage, diced (4 cups)
- 1 cup wasabi peas
- 1 cup dry roasted edamame
- 2 cups dried pineapple
- 2 tablespoons dried parsley (optional)

Properly balanced, homemade trail mixes provide pocket fuel for high-energy activities.

Put everything in a large, clean bag and shake gently to mix. Package in snack bags by the cupful. Keep in a cool, dry place and use within two weeks.

NOSEBAG GORP

MAKES 14 CUPS

Like a horse's nosebag, this snack is heavy on oats and other highly nourishing ingredients.

- 12 cups of unsalted popcorn, picked over
- 1½ cups rolled oats (one-minute or old-fashioned)
- 1 cup peanuts
- ½ cup butter, butter-flavor shortening, or butter-flavor vegetable oil
- 2 tablespoons additional vegetable oil
- ⅔ cup packed brown sugar
- ⅓ cup honey
- ½ teaspoon each salt, vanilla

Make popcorn and set it aside. Heat oats and nuts in an oven or dry skillet just until toasty. They'll taste better and will also mix more easily because they are warm. Use nonstick spray to coat a very large pot or a clean dishpan.

Add popcorn. In a medium pan, heat butter, oil, salt, and honey and bring to a boil. When it boils count 90 seconds on the clock. (That's 1 minute, 30 seconds.) Stir in vanilla.

Carefully drizzle the syrup over the popcorn, using a sprayed spatula to mix well. Stir in warm oats and nuts. Press mixture into sprayed pan(s) and cool completely. Break into pieces.

PINE NUT GORP

MAKES 26 HALF-CUP PORTIONS

Pine nuts, also called pignoli, are pricey, but they have a flavor like no other. They make a healthful homemade gorp. The only cooking is toasting the pine nuts and making the popcorn (preferably hot air popped with no oil or salt).

> 1 cup pine nuts
>
> 2 cups whole almonds
>
> 2 cups pecan halves
>
> 8 cups plain popcorn
>
> 2 tablespoons garlic salt

Toast pine nuts in a dry skillet, shaking constantly over high heat until they are golden. Watch carefully so they don't burn. Cool completely. Mix everything in a large bag and scoop out by the cupful to seal in snack bags. Keep cool and dry. A cupful with a beverage makes a meal; a half cup is a good snack.

PURPLE PEOPLE EATER GORP

MAKES 18 CUPS

This one is for kids who love grape soda, messy snacks, and purple tongues.

> 12 cups plain popcorn
>
> 1 packet dry grape-flavored gelatin dessert mix (regular or sugar-free)
>
> 2 packages dry Acai Emergen-C drink mix
>
> 2 cups snipped moist dried plums
>
> 2 cups snipped dried figs or pitted dates
>
> 2 cups raisins

Put the popcorn and moist dried plums in a large, clean bag with the gelatin and Emergen-C. Shake gently. Add dried fruit, seal bag, and shake again to mix thoroughly. Pack in snack bags by the cupful. Makes 18 portions of a cupful each.

SALMON GORP

MAKES 13 CUPS

Dried wild salmon nuggets are tasty and nutritious, but the taste is so strong and the protein so concentrated that a little goes a long way. Make a more balanced meal by drinking plenty of liquids and eating this gorp with items high in fiber. Cured salmon is usually very salty, so dilute it with low- or no-salt ingredients.

   2 cups dried wild salmon nuggets, cut up if necessary

   4 cups popped popcorn

   2 cups parched corn snack food

   2 cups dried fruit (pineapple tidbits, dried cherries, raisins)

   2 cups salt-free, bite-size pretzels

   1 cup wasabi peas

Combine everything in a large bag and toss gently to mix well. Seal in snack bags by the cupful. Makes 13 servings of one cup each. Keep in a cool, dry place.

Salmon nuggets have provisioned travelers since ancient times.

Chapter 12

Freezer Failures, Fires, and Floods

The Big Thaw

Most householders and many boaters and RV-ers store a major portion of their food supply in a freezer, but that means exposure to mechanical failures, power outages, freak accidents, and mischief. A weekender returned to her camp to find that other campers had unplugged her RV because they wanted the hookup for themselves. A hunter may return to his cabin to find that a squirrel had paid with its life for gnawing through a power cord. Now 200 pounds of venison are starting to thaw!

During some hurricanes and other natural disasters, homes may be without electricity for weeks. Even if you have propane refrigeration, a popular option for people who live off-grid, there can be propane shortages because of strikes or road closures. Our friends in the Bahamas were caught short of gas for their stove and refrigerator when the freight boat had to go into the boatyard for a month.

On a boat or RV, where most refrigeration systems are non-standard, things get more complicated. Most modern RV refrigerators work on both household and 12-volt power, with a variety of backups such as a generator, solar panels, wind generator, inverter with battery bank, and so on. Three-way RV refrigerators work on 110V, 12V, or propane. Many boat refrigeration systems have an engine-driven compressor, usually with a eutectic plate that holds the cold so the compressor needs to run only two or three times a day. Boats may also rely on solar and other power sources.

Nevertheless, stuff happens.

The late Don and Sue Moesly, who wrote *Circumnavigating: Sail the Trade Winds* in two volumes (Wescott Cove Publishing), sailed around the world on board their 38-foot sailboat *Svea*. Their refrigeration was powered by shore power and, when they were at sea, by an engine-driven compressor. Then they lost their engine when they were in the Indian Ocean, many days from port. Able sailors, they set their canvas for safe harbor several

Freezer Triage: Salvaging Your Stores

As soon as you realize the problem, it's triage time. Open the freezer as infrequently as possible. Eat or preserve frozen foods as soon as possible. The old adage "Life begins at 40" is based on 40 degrees Fahrenheit. That's when organisms begin to grow in earnest. Some chefs now keep foods below that, in the high 30s.

One or more of the following plans might suit your food preparedness situation:

- If you may face a freezer failure at home, find out if any dry ice or food lockers are available nearby. Know how to get quick shipment of spare parts for your brand and model refrigerator. If you have a standby generator, keep it in tune and know how to hook it up to the refrigerator or freezer.
- Booklets on preserving methods are available from your county home extension home economist. Follow them carefully when the time comes.
- A pressure canner is a plus, but I have also canned many pints and half-pints in four- and six-quart pressure cookers. Keep empty jars and extra lids on hand. Water bath canning isn't recommended for meat, fish, or low-acid vegetables.
- Download plans for making a simple solar dehydrator and keep them handy.
- It takes little room to stow a supply of preservatives such as sugar, vinegar, and pickling salt (do not use iodized table salt). As the freezer thaws, fruits can be made into jam, vegetables pickled, baked goods dried.
- Meats and seafood can be canned, cured, or smoked. Special curing salt is sold for meat. Known as Pink Prague or Prague Powder, it contains sodium nitrate or sodium nitrite plus pink dye and agents that promote curing. Morton's Tender Quick, found in most supermarkets, is another curing substance containing salt, sugar, and other ingredients.
- If the power returns, it's generally said to be safe to cook or re-freeze foods if they still contain some ice crystals.

days away, but their refrigeration was dead in the water. Fortunately Sue had a pressure cooker and a supply of canning jars to save a costly supply of meat.

About Floods

Did your bilge or basement flood, contaminating stowed food supplies? If the flood was a river or urban run-off, it's filled with chemical and biological filth. Even if it was clean sea water, corrosive forces are already at work. Aluminum cans are eaten through in a few hours and steel is starting to rust.

Retrieve cans and jars that are still sealed and intact, but discard jars that have plastic lids and cardboard inner liners (such as peanut butter and mayonnaise). Pitch everything else including eggs (even if they are not broken), produce including unpeeled fruit and vegetables, and paper labels from canned goods. Use a grease pencil to relabel cans you can identify.

If your garden was under dirty water for some hours, leafy crops should be discarded but root vegetables might be washed and peeled depending on whether flood waters were highly contaminated.

Using a bleach solution (2 tablespoons per gallon of water) or other sanitizing wash, immerse any undamaged cans and jars for 10 minutes. Rinse thoroughly in fresh water. Dry them to prevent rust. Remove metal rings from home-canned jars. If the seal is unbroken and contents intact, wash the outsides of the jars and rings. Dry well and replace rings to protect the seal.

Food and Fires

Even if the stowed food in your cabin, home, RV, or boat appears to survive a fire, there are good reasons to be wary. In addition to power outage damage to refrigerated and frozen foods, you're also dealing with damage from excess heat, smoke, including toxic fumes, and chemical contamination from fire extinguishing agents.

Sealed cans and jars that look unscathed are probably safe to eat, but if they were exposed to extreme heat spoilage is accelerated even inside the can. Use foods as soon as possible and only if they look and taste normal. Raw foods such as potatoes and melons, and food packaged in porous materials such as plastic, paper, and cardboard may have been subjected to toxic fumes from burning furniture and building materials. Even if they were in a refrigerator or freezer, discard them if they smell odd.

Not all firefighting chemicals are toxic to the touch, but they are messy and corrosive, and shouldn't be consumed. Wash all canned food, tableware, pots, and pans that were

Having a backup generator is always a plus, but it's important to keep it maintained and fueled.

exposed. Use hot, soapy water, then soak in a bleach solution for 10 to 20 minutes. Rinse and dry.

Bottom line: when in doubt, throw it out—and discard it in a place where pets and wildlife can't eat it.

Gear for the Prepared Pantry

Are you suddenly without electricity? Running short of fuel? On limited water rations or otherwise relying on a backup plan? These items might come in handy. If you always live off-grid, you may also want a hand-operated blender to make purées and baby food, a manual grain mill, and a solar dehydrator and solar cooker. They're all available online.

Mortar and Pestle

Why: Stone tools provide an effective manual way to grind grains, seeds, nuts, beans, and spices.

Pro: Thousands of years and countless cultures have proven the value of this primitive hand tool in meal preparation. Many seeds and pods release their best flavor when freshly ground.

Con: Heavy weight is a minus for camping or boating

Piezo Sparker

Why: Start a gas flame with a spark.

Pro: Featherweight. Lasts forever. You'll still need matches or a butane light to create flame to light tinder, wicks, and liquid alcohol, but this sparker lasts forever and needs no batteries or cartridges.

Con: Creates only a spark, so it works only with gaseous fuels.

Pressure Cooker

Why: Multipurpose cookers can be used with or without pressure as a cooker, oven, steamer, and canner. Saves time and fuel. In many applications it's faster than a microwave.

Many cooks prepare their own spice blends for good reasons. Whole seeds and pods do not release their peak flavor until they are ground.

For example, one baked potato nukes in four minutes; 10 potatoes take 40 minutes. In a pressure cooker potatoes take about the same time whether you're cooking one or a dozen.

Pro: A lifetime investment that many chefs use every day. Can be used on conventional burner or solid-fuel stove.

Con: May involve a learning curve. Using other than as directed can be dangerous. Rubber parts eventually degrade and need replacement.

Seed Sprouter Lid for a Mason Jar

Why: Seeds can be stored for months and even years, then brought back to nutritious life within a few days by adding water. With a proper sprouter rather than makeshift means, you avoid waste that results from using too much or too little water. Larger, stackable sprouters are available for serious sprouters, but they're too bulky to stow for emergency use.

Pro: Lightweight, compact to store until needed. Simple to use, fits standard jars. Buy several to keep your "garden" going.

Con: There is a learning curve regarding all the available types of seeds, how to sprout them, and how to use them in meals.

Double Gear Can Opener

Why: The best manual can openers are gear driven, giving you power to open large cans and cans with lost keys or broken pull rings. This is one of the most important tools in the pantry, so keep a spare can opener with emergency supplies.

Pro: Inexpensive, available anywhere. Requires less strength than friction-drive can openers.

Con: The cutting edge rusts in time but is easily cleaned.

A Campfire Corn Popper

Why: Popcorn is a natural, nutritious food that stores compactly yet swells to create delicious desserts and snacks. It's in the Top Ten of stowaway food essentials.

Pro: Works over any heat source.

Con: If you've never made popcorn except in the microwave, you'll need some practice.

Insulated Containers

Why: To conserve energy, use insulation to keep things hotter or colder. Bonus points if the ice chest is large and strong enough to resist vermin and animals. A wide-mouth thermos bottle can hold hot water all day or carry soup or coffee for the trail.

Pro: Multiple uses. Choose an ice chest with a flat top to use as a seat or work surface. It's good to keep foods dry, wet, colder, warmer. It keeps bread dough warm and out of the wind while it rises. Heavily lined with additional pillows, newspaper, or other insulation, an ice chest serves as a fireless cooker. Bring soaked beans to boiling in the morning, surround with heavy insulation and the beans are ready by dinner time. A wide-mouth thermos can be used for solid foods, not just liquids. An unbreakable, stainless steel thermos is a lifetime investment.

Con: Insulated containers in any size are bulkier than non insulated containers.

Instant-Read Thermometer

Why: Food safety is job one. The old rule of "keep it hot or keep it cold" applies. Even if foods were prepared from preserved ingredients, they must be kept hot enough or cold enough to keep bacteria at bay. Now used widely by home cooks as well as food inspectors, these thermometers are easily found in supermarkets and kitchen supply stores. Some are pocket- size.

Pro: You'll know at once when foods pass out of the safety zone.

Con: Must be used correctly. Some sensors are instant; some take a second or more to report accurately.

Grain Mill

Why: Freshly ground grains, cereals, seeds, and coffee beans are at the top of their game, nutrition-wise and taste-wise. Makeshift means of grinding, such as a high-powered blender, grind unevenly. Sifting is required to avoid tooth-cracking surprises. A proper grain mill is essential.

Pro: A must in the kitchen for those who want freshly ground wheat. Models come in manual, electric, or convertible operation. (Convertibles can be used manually when the power is out.) Stone burrs crush the grain, metal burrs break it, and impact mills pound the grain into fine flour.

Con: The best ones are expensive. Manual mills require time and elbow grease. Learn correct usage so you don't overheat flour, destroying nutrients.

Water Supplies

The well goes dry. Your home's water supply stops when a water main breaks or there is a toxic chemical spill.

What if you're suddenly without water for drinking or cooking? If your faucet water is toxic due to a chemical spill or algae bloom, you can't even use it for showering. Your backup plans will depend on your lifestyle. On a seagoing boat you might add a solar distillation unit. If you live near a clean river or lake you might have a UV water purifier or a filter-chlorinator water treatment device. At your house or apartment you might just stash a case of two of bottled water. Survival gear suppliers offer many storage and treatment options, but let's keep it simple. Have one or more of these backups available.

Collapsible Jugs

Why: In a water emergency you may have to tote water from the nearest river, main, relief supply truck, or well.

Pro: Stored empty, these jugs take up almost no space at all. Forget them until you need them. Easily available at home centers and camping supply stores.

Con: Limited life span, especially if stored in hot, dry places. Plastics break down from heat, light, and flexing.

Rain Barrel

Why: It's a plus to save roof run-off any time for watering the garden or washing the car. In emergencies it's suitable for flushing the toilet, doing laundry, and bathing.

Pro: A renewable way to have a standby water supply.

Con: Not for arid areas. Water not suitable for drinking if it contains leaves, bird droppings, or debris from shingles.

Bottled Water

Why: The obvious way for the casual prepper to keep extra water on hand.

Pro: Buy at any supermarket, drug store, or big-box retailer. Affordable. Use-by dated. Both filtered/purified and distilled water are available in gallon jugs. After use, gallon jugs can be useful for toting water from other sources.

Con: Bulky. Shelf life is long but not unlimited. Distilled water does not contain vital minerals.

Rain Water Catchment

Why: In many parts of the world where wells are sparse and rains irregular, large land areas are paved and sloped to channel water into cisterns or other storage facilities.

How: The roofs of your home and outbuildings are probably the largest catchment on your property. A large driveway or tennis court might also be utilized. On a smaller scale, the same concept can work on an RV roof or boat deck. Simply design a way to capture the water and channel it to a reservoir.

You don't need a large area or hard surface. A tarp or awning can be rigged to catch water in your back yard, patio, campsite, or boat deck. On our sailboat we put a hose fitting in the middle of the canvas sun shade. When it rained, we just lowered the topping lift so the shade would form a catchment, then hooked up a hose that channeled rain water into a jug.

Choosing a Spare Stove

For many householders the patio propane grill is a primary backup to the kitchen stove. In fact, you may use it almost every day. No other backup stove is needed. The fuel supply is easily backed up with a second propane tank, and a hooded grill can do almost anything the kitchen stove can do. As a second stove it's far preferable to a charcoal grill, which uses a bulky fuel that produces fewer BTUs per dollar, per pound, and per cubic foot.

Fuel

For convenience, get a backup stove that uses a fuel you have on hand anyway. In many areas, wood can be picked up anywhere. Small propane cylinders are easy to keep on hand and they can be used in workshop tools, lanterns, stoves, and heaters. It's also easy to keep spare cartridges on hand for the butane buffet burner you use for buffets and picnics.

Solid fuel (Sterno, ThermaFuel) is found in supermarkets and it's easy to store. A solar cooker is the ultimate backup anywhere the sun shines. Wood pellets are a fast-growing segment of the alternative fuel marketplace. Coleman makes a camp stove that can be fueled with either white gas or unleaded auto gas.

So-called alternative fuel stoves may be slow to heat, but they can cook with odd bits and pieces such as sticks and dry leaves.

Keep in mind that all fuels must be handled with kid gloves for safety's

Keep extra fuel on hand for the backyard gas grill, the ultimate backup stove.
(Weber Grills)

sake. Some fuels evaporate or degrade (microbes grow in kerosene/diesel fuel; wood rots when wet). Disposable fuel cartridges and cylinders are convenient but are bulky and a disposal problem. Liquid fuels are awkward to handle and heavy to transport. Fumes or smoke can range from unpleasant to extremely dangerous. Odorless, invisible carbon monoxide is a notorious killer. All combustion uses oxygen and creates moisture, so not all stoves can be used in an enclosure.

Auxiliary Stove Considerations

Once you decide on what fuel(s) are best for your emergency stove, also consider the following:

- How stable is the cooker itself? Some folding camp stoves are too flimsy to handle a pot of water, yet boiling drinking water may be the most important task your backup stove must do in an emergency. The stove should sit solidly on the ground or other surface and also provide a solid seat for the cooking pot.

- How easy is it to operate? Some camp stoves have built-in ignition. Others must be pumped up to create pressure, preheated or periodically fitted with new wicks or batteries. Some wood pellet stoves, heaters, and water heaters require a household electrical outlet.
- Will you use this stove often for other purposes? If not, what problems are involved in storing the fuel and the stove itself? Steel rusts, gaskets and o-rings deteriorate, batteries die and corrode. In an RV, boat, or small apartment, size matters.
- Suitable cookware should be available for the stove. Thin aluminum pots come up to temperature quicker, but heavier pots hold heat longer. Dark pots absorb solar heat better.
- Many stoves, including some marine and camping models, have one or more regular burners plus a "blower" burner for quicker heating. It consumes fuel faster but is a plus for stir-frying and heating water.
- It's difficult to regulate heat on most emergency stoves. Setting a very low flame often puts out the fire completely. Add a flame tamer, also called a flame spreader, to your emergency gear to aid in stove-top baking and making delicate sauces.

How to Bake Without an Oven

Whether you're ashore or afloat, this book assumes you'll have one or more alternative ways to cook. Since many emergency stoves don't have an oven, and you may want a loaf of bread or a birthday cake, here is my Plan B.

When I told friends that I'd be living on a small sailboat with a two-burner Primus stove and no oven, an older friend gave me valuable advice. Years ago her husband went on the road to sell a line of cast aluminum cookware and bakeware. Back then, many kitchens had iron cookstoves. In summer, when it was too hot to fire up with wood or coal, country cooks used kerosene burners. These "summer stoves" were fine for stewing, frying, and canning, but they had no ovens. Cast aluminum bakeware was an easy sell because it could bake atop a burner.

When you're baking over a small burner it's essential to use a heavy pan, such as cast aluminum, that conducts heat readily. Although cast iron is a good choice for campfires and grates, where pots sit on a wide bed of coals, iron develops hot spots over a small camp stove burner. To make breads and cakes, you want to replicate a conventional oven with even heat on the bottom, sides, and top.

My two stove-top "ovens" are a cast aluminum pressure cooker with rubber rings and gaskets removed, and a 12-inch cast aluminum skillet with matching cast aluminum lid.

The Indirect Method

Simply use the pan as you would an oven. The pan should be very clean and dry. Do not grease it. Any soil or grease will bake on and may even burn, smoke, and ruin the food. Put a shallow rack in the bottom to promote heat flow. Preheat the covered pan over high heat. Put the batter, dough, or casserole in its own greased or nonstick pan and quickly put it in the hot "oven." Keep heat high and don't let heat escape by removing the lid often.

Because the "oven" cavity is small there is more moisture. Casseroles won't brown or develop a crusty top. However, there are fixes. Skillet-toasted bread crumbs make a crusty topping over a pale casserole. I've also used a kitchen torch to brown a topping.

With practice you'll soon develop a nose and a sense for timing, heat management, and adapting recipes for stove-top baking. With the indirect method, the skillet or pressure cooker remains clean and ready to use again.

The Direct Method

It's riskier to bake right on the surface of the pan, but it also makes a better crust. Start with a cold, lightly greased (preferably cast aluminum) skillet or pressure cooker. Remove the pressure cooker's rubber gasket. You aren't raising pressure but are simply creating a cavity where heat will surround the product evenly.

When baking bread, biscuits, or pizza, grease heavily with solid shortening and scatter cornmeal on the surface for a crisper crust. Put batter or dough in the cold skillet. (If baking yeast bread, put dough in the pan for its final rising.) Cover the pan tightly or lock on the pressure cooker lid and place the pan over low-medium heat.

From here on it's guesswork. You can't peek often, but you also don't want the food to burn on the bottom. Some cooks turn bread or meatloaf halfway through. I don't. When it's done I just turn it out on the cutting board with the pale side down.

Use your sense of smell and learn by experience depending on your stove, your pans, and your recipes.

Tips on Solar Cooking

* Follow any directions that came with your solar cooker.
* Each model or homemade design has its own quirks for use and care. Surfaces that are transparent or reflective can dull over time, reducing efficiency. Protect them from damage.
* If the cooker doesn't have a built-in temperature gauge, add an inexpensive oven thermometer. Temperatures above 40°F and below 120°F simply invite food poisoning.
* It's always a plus if you can jump-start the cooking process by preheating the cooker itself and also

heating any foods or liquids to be cooked. For example, you might soak beans overnight, cover them in boiling water, and then put them in the preheated solar cooker.

Three Ways to Cook Rice

Every cook has a favorite way of cooking rice. Rice gourmets also have preferred methods for each different type of rice. When you're saving fuel, or don't have enough burners, or don't have household power to use your trusty rice cooker, try one of these methods.

1. To cook rice off the burner, bring one part rice and two parts water or broth to a boil in a pressure cooker. Raise full pressure, remove from heat, and put the cooker in a wind-free spot while pressure returns to normal. When it does, fluff rice with a fork and serve.
2. Using a wide-mouth thermos or other thermal container, preheat the container with a little boiling water. Discard this water and put in one part boiling water per one part instant rice. Seal thermos and tip gently to mix. Let stand for up to an hour. Spoon out hot, perfectly cooked rice.
3. To improvise a rice steamer, shape a "bowl" out of aluminum foil. Fill a pan with a couple inches of water. While water heats, put one part raw, regular rice and one part water in the "bowl." Cover and boil until rice is tender. Normal rice cooking requires two parts water to one part rice, but with this method the extra moisture is provided by the steam. The result is a tender, fluffy, just-right rice. Lift out the foil and nothing is left in the pan but clean, hot water.

Substitutions, Fakes, and Look-alikes

Baking Powder—To make most cakes and other baked goods rise without baking powder, use ½ teaspoon baking soda and 1 tablespoon vinegar per 2 cups flour. Add soda with dry ingredients; mix vinegar with the wet ingredients.

Cream Cheese—See yogurt, below. Make yogurt, then drain it until it's thick (Greek style yogurt, sour cream) or thicker (cream cheese).

Eggs—Mix a tablespoon of ground flax seeds with 3 tablespoons water until mixture is thick. Use in recipes in place of one egg. This recipe is mostly of interest to vegans or people who are allergic to eggs. Fresh and powdered eggs are preferred. They're affordable and easy to keep on hand.

Eggplant—There's no substitute for fresh eggplant, but pickled and fried eggplant are available in cans and jars in supermarkets that sell Middle Eastern staples. Both have their place in cuisine. Caponata (Italian eggplant appetizer) is also available in cans.

Ketchup—Combine a 6-ounce can of tomato paste with ¼ cup each vinegar and brown sugar. Stir in ½ teaspoon cinnamon and

¼ teaspoon cloves. Optional: add a little Worcestershire or soy sauce.

Milk, Evaporated Nonfat—Combine 1 cup nonfat milk powder and 1 cup water. Stir to dissolve. Let stand 1 to 2 hours.

Milk, Nonfat—Scant 1 quart water plus 1⅔ cup nonfat dry milk powder. For the best consistency, let steep for 2 to 3 hours in a cool place.

Milk, Sweetened condensed—Canned condensed milk has two special properties. First, it can be turned into pudding or pie filling simply by adding lemon or lime juice, which "sets" the milk. Second, it can be steamed in the open can until it caramelizes, forming a candy or sauce. To make your own condensed milk combine one cup instant nonfat dry milk and ⅔ cup sugar. Stir into ⅓ cup boiling water. Optional: add a tablespoon of melted butter.

Mustard—It can be fun and creative to invent your own mustards to add a

Time-honored black iron cookware is ideal for cooking over an oven fire, but it isn't always the best for a camp stove and other emergency cookers. (South Carolina Tourism)

kick to bland meals from the pantry. Start with a mixture of 3 parts powdered dry mustard to 1 part each water, vinegar, and sugar. Vary the mustard by using different vinegars, different sweeteners, and/or additions such as ground hazelnuts, coarsely chopped walnuts, rehydrated diced onion, or garlic granules. Try using white wine instead of the water and vinegar.

Pancake Syrup—Boil 2 cups sugar with 1 cup water and stir in 1 teaspoon maple flavoring such as Mapleine. Maple extract can also be stirred into corn syrup, 1 teaspoon per cupful.

Saffron—Turmeric is sometimes used, measure for measure, in place of the far more costly saffron.

Simple Syrup—Bring two parts sugar and one part water to a boil. Simple syrup is an essential ingredient in many bar drinks, some recipes, and authentic Southern sweet tea.

Thickening Agents—Cooks generally thicken sauces and gravies with flour or cornstarch but dozens of other agents may be used. Most should be dissolved in cold water first, usually at the rate of 1 tablespoon thickener per cup of liquid, Stir, heating until it thickens. Alternative thickeners include cornmeal, polenta, a wide range of non wheat flours, tapioca, potato starch, arrowroot, and agar, a seaweed derivative that is often used to make dessert puddings and gels. Instant potato flakes or oatmeal can be used to thicken hot foods, but use a light and patient hand. Sprinkle over hot soup one tablespoon at a time, stir and cook, then add more if needed.

Some dishes require eggs to thicken or "set" them. This requires heat, such as when baking a quiche or cooking an omelet. When using dehydrated eggs it's important to use eggs that reconstitute to a liquid. Some freeze-dried eggs are already cooked. Add hot water and you have an omelet, but since these eggs are already cooked they won't work in a custard pie.

Yeast—There is no substitute for yeast in bread making. It's a living, breathing organism, picky about its environment and tricky to keep alive. Fortunately it's in the air all around us and with luck and patience you can capture it. Try mixing 1¼ cup unbleached flour with a cup of warm water. Cover the bowl with clean cloth and let it stand until it forms a bubbly batter, usually after 24 to 48 hours. This then becomes the basis for a batch of yeast bread, although some of the sourdough can be saved and "fed" with more water and flour to use in the next batch of bread.

The easiest way to begin is with commercial yeast. Observe use-by dates. Entire books are written on sourdough management and bread making, so we don't go into it further.

Yogurt—Like yeast, yogurt is a live culture that is selective about its care and feeding. It can be propagated by inoculating warm milk with a little of the old yogurt. Milk should not be disturbed during the process, which usually takes 6 to 12 hours.

Zucchini—Fresh zucchini and summer squash are mostly water. They can be dehydrated, frozen, or canned, but cannot be restored to any semblance of the original. Canned zucchini in tomato sauce is available on supermarket shelves.

Equivalents

These measures are mere guidelines. Professional chefs use weight rather than volume.

One pound of	Measure
Bread flour	3⅓ cups
Butter	2 cups
Coffee	5 cups
Cornmeal	2⅔ cups
Cornstarch	3¼ cups
Eggs	8 whole or 10 broken
Egg whites	1 cup
Egg yolks	16
Farina	2⅓ cups
Flour, soft	4 cups
Lard, shortening	2 cups
Raisins	2 cups
Rice	2 cups
Rolled oats	5⅓ cups
Sugar	2 cups
Tea, loose	5½ cups

Recommended Resources

The purpose of this book is to make your neighborhood supermarket your primary source for provisions. In addition, these companies may be of interest.

http://www.amazon.com
You probably already know that Amazon has one of the planet's best selections of foods, survival gear, kitchen essentials, and equipment for camping and boating.

http://www.amishfoods.com
Amish tradition has evolved, but the folks from Lancaster, Pennsylvania, who sell their wholesome, Amish-made meats, cheeses, and preserves online, know a thing or two about shelf-stable foods.

http://www.beprepared.com
Find storage foods, survival foods, water purification, solar cookers, and countless options to inspire your trip or emergency plans. (800) 999-1863

http://www.campingworld.com
This RV specialist also has retail stores throughout North America. 800-626-3636

http://www.costco.com
You never know what you'll find! Watch for freeze-dried and shelf-stable staples. 800-955-2292

http://www.cruisersforum.com
Join this online, global community of sailors to exchange tips on all aspects of boat life including provisioning and food preparation.

https://www.gopresto.com
Find pressure cookers and canners, plus information on pressure canning. 800-877-0441

http://www.maxlifefoods.com
You can use this company's preparedness calculator to figure out just what you need! 888-858-6387

http://www.preparewise.com
Amazing selection of volume quantity survival food and water systems, plus non-GMO and gluten-free samplers. 888-545-6265

http://www.samsclub.com
Another vast resource—great for larger-scale group planning. 888-746-7726

http://www.walmart.com
Yep, they're everywhere, and offer emergency food supplies as well as almost everything else.

http://www.werlingandsons.com
This Ohio farm specializes in canned meats. (888) 375-1998

http://www.westmarine.com
Retail stores and online sales of marine quality galley gear, safety equipment, water treatments, and related supplies. (855) 894-9869

http://www.wisefoodstorage.com
Bulk everything. Check out this website's "Prepping for Disaster" infographic. 800-393-2570

Index

About the Author

Janet Groene writes several columns that run regularly in *Family Motor Coaching* magazine (145,000 members of FMCA) and in *Houseboat* magazine. Janet has loyal followers for her blogs on travel, RV cooking, boat cooking, and SoloWomanRV. She holds the Distinguished Achievement in RV Journalism Award and the NMMA Direcotrs Award for boating journalism, and she is a member of the American Society of Journalists & Authors, Boating Writers International, and the Society of American Travel Writers. She works fulltime as a freelance travel writer.

For ten years, Janet Groene and her late husband, Gordon, lived fulltime on the go by sailboat and camper. Magazine assignments have taken Groene worldwide, where she provisioned locally to travel in bareboats and rental campers of many types and sizes. Her home base is now in rural North Florida.

Having traveled widely in a small sailboat and camper, Janet Groene knows how to make big meals using pantry foods and minimum space.